THE WORLD OF
FORMULA ONE

Written by
Michael O'Neill

sb sona
BOOKS

sona
BOOKS

© Danann Media Publishing Ltd 2022

First published in the UK 2022 by Sona Books an imprint of Danann Media Publishing Ltd

CAT NO: SON0519

Photography courtesy of

Getty images:

- Dan Istitene
- Mark Thompson
- Adrian Dennis/AFP
- Lars Baron
- Peter J Fox
- Ben Stansall/Pool
- Dan Mullan - Formula 1
- Dimitri lundt/Corbis/VCG
- Giuseppe Cacace - Pool
- Charles Coates
- Miguel Medina/AFP
- Clive Rose
- Bryn Lennon
- Vladimir Rys Photography
- Hoch Zwei/Corbis
- Dimitar Dilkoff/AFP
- Jewel Samad/AFP
- Rudy Carezzevoli
- Mario Renzi - Formula 1
- Alexander Hassenstein/Bongarts

Alamy images:

- dpa picture alliance
- James Moy
- Evren Kalinbacak
- Obstando Images

Book layout & design Darren Grice at Ctrl-d
Copy editor Tom O'Neill

Made in EU.

ISBN: 978-1-912918-92-8

CONTENTS

THE WORLD OF
FORMULA ONE

The mere mention of their names sets the pulses of aficionados... well, racing, of course: Lewis Hamilton, Sebastian Vettel, Max Verstappen, Michael Schumacher, Damon Hill, Emerson Fittipaldi, Fernando Alonso, Jochen Rindt, James Hunt – and for those with longer memories, the incomparable Juan Manuel Fangio, gentleman Graham Hill and the inimitable Ayrton Senna. And for the younger generation of fans, we have Lando Norris, Lance Stroll and Charles Leclerc. These are the gods of the Formula One racing circuits, the darlings of the stands, and they cause vast quantities of adrenaline to be pumped through the hearts of millions of fans glued to their TV sets each week or rigid in the circuits of the stands as two hours of thrills, rivalries and, sadly though miraculously rarely, tragedies unfold during the Formula One racing season.

The Formula One drivers of today are known far beyond the finishing line of the Grand Prix circuits, which have become almost as renowned as the drivers; Monaco, Silverstone, Brands Hatch, Nurburgring, Autodromo Nazionale di Monza or the Hockenheimring in Germany, and countries eagerly compete to host this colourful circus of teams, their star engineers and their family and technical entourages.

For the teams and the constructors of their high-tech cars, too, there is glory and fame to be gained by a sleek machine hurtling down the final straight and across the finish line ahead of the pack. A Mercedes, a Ferrari, a Renault or a Red Bull Racing Honda can bask in the limelight of victory and add sheen and prestige to their reputations – and hope that the adoration of fans will transform into sales in their car showrooms across the globe.

So let's delve into this intriguing and fascinating world of Formula One, let's see who the favourites are whose ice-cool temperaments enable them to accelerate to 60 mph from a standing start in 2.6 seconds and hit speeds of 231.4 mph (achieved by Valtteri Bottas, currently world record holder for the highest speed during an F1 race), the circuits they conquer and the expert teams who support them and their fine-tuned, shiny steeds.

THE DRIVERS

As the men behind the steering wheels are the heroes of the sport, it's seems only fair to start with them. And as perhaps the greatest driver in the contemporary history of the sport, Lewis Hamilton arguably deserves his first past the flag on this occasion in the list of contemporary F1 pilots.

F1 is awash with rivalries between drivers, some of which have led to serious incidents on the track that have endangered driver's lives and not only those of the feuding parties. Who can ever forget the Ayrton Senna – Alain Prost clashes that almost killed them both. Lewis Hamilton and Nico Rosberg behaved equally recklessly, colliding in 2014 in Belgium, which is what happened to Sebastian Vettel and Mark Webber in Turkey. And for those with longer memories there was the James Hunt/Niki Lauda clash in 1976, the year Lauda was almost killed. And of course, the infamous Damon Hill contra Michael Schumacher that caused dangerous collisions and bitter accusations.

LE

HAMILTON

Sir Lewis Carl Davidson Hamilton MBE HonFREng (Fellowship of the Royal Academy of Engineering). Driving for his country, the United Kingdom, Lewis was born on the 7th of January 1985 in Stevenage, Hertfordshire.

Let's say it now, he is the most successful racing driver of all time and certainly of his generation; seven times world champion having tied with Michael Schumacher with 7 world championships but holding the F1 record for race victories standing at 103 since winning the Saudi Arabian GP in 2021 and having gained the most pole positions and the most podiums. And a fact not to be underestimated, the first-ever black Formula 1 driver.

Raised in the Catholic faith by his father, Anthony Hamilton, whose family hails from Grenada in Central America, and his mother Carmen Larbalestier, his parents separated when he was two years old. Lewis went to live with his mother until he was twelve, after which he moved back to live with his father and Linda, his stepmother, and half-brother Nicolas, also a professional racing driver.

Sadly, even at The John Henry Newman School, a Catholic secondary school, the five-year-old Hamilton was already subjected to bullying, which led him to learn karate for self protection.

Lewis spent a lot of time with his father and loved visiting the Go-Kart tracks with him. The young driver began karting in 1993, and his talent was soon on display as he won race after race. Anthony did his utmost to encourage and support his son's passion in the sport. For example, Anthony left his job as an IT manager and worked at four different jobs – dishwasher, double glazing salesman, and putting up estate agents' signs amongst them. He would repair old karts into the early hours of the morning in his garage and yet still attend his son's races and remained Lewis's manager until 2010. And it was the dedication of father and son that led to Lewis winning his first national championship at the age of ten.

It was to prove a life-changing victory, for Lewis met Ron Dennis, founder and president of the British McLaren team – telling him, "One day I want to be racing your cars" – with whom he signed a contract in 1998, at 13 years of age, the youngest driver to ever have signed for an F1 team. It was confidence well placed, for Lewis, the lad with the "youthful, naive, warm personality", proved to be a winner.

Lewis began his long climb up the ladder to F1 driving in the Intercontinental A in 1999, the Formula A in 2000 – the year he became European Champion by gaining maximum points. It was also the year in which the British Racing Drivers' Club

rewarded his karting success by making him a 'Rising Star' member. One year later, in 2001, during the Formula Super A, he was given praise from on high – by Michael Schumacher no less.

Changing to the ASM team for 2005, he was victorious in 15 of the 20 races, dominating the European F3, and the following year was in GP2, now Formula 2, with ART to produce one of the most impressive performances ever seen. It was obvious to everyone around him that it was time for Lewis to join the big boys.

LEWIS HAMILTON RACE STATS

288 GRAND PRIX 103 WINS (35.76%) 4,165.50 POINTS 5,796 LAPS LED 103 POLE POSITIONS 59 FASTEST LAPS 182 PODIUMS 19 HAT TRICKS 6 GRAND SLAMS 27 RETIREMENTS 17,326 LAPS RACED 82,800 KM RACED 15 SEASONS (2007-2021) 5 TEAMMATES (FERNANDO ALONSO, HEIKI KOVALAINEN, JENSON BUTTON, NICO ROSBERG, VALTTERI BOTTAS).

In 2007, alongside a – it must be said, very reluctant Fernando Alonso – Lewis appeared in his first F1 race, and one year later at the age of 23, he brought home his first victory for McLaren. The rookie that Alonso had derided was on the podium consecutively for his first nine races, and the discontent at McLaren was soon palpable. An irate Alonso then blocked Hamilton in the pits in a final qualifying round in an ill-fated attempt to force Ron Dennis, McLaren's Formula One team boss, to accept Fernando's status as number one in the stable; to no avail. Neither was Lewis prepared to play second fiddle to anyone, even the man who was one of F1's top drivers, his teammate Fernando Alonso.

It was at Monaco that Lewis refused to slow down on team instructions; that was the beginning of the end. Alonso did all he could to disadvantage his teammate, but Lewis was as ruthlessly ambitious as anyone and determined that no one, not even his team, was going to stop him, displaying the steely character that would take him to championships time and time again. McLaren's test driver at the time, De la Rosa, said that what separated Lewis and Alonso from the rest was simple: "Pure, raw talent".

With Alonso gone for 2008, Lewis began his rise to F1 superstardom with a last-gasp win, overtaking Timo Glock on the final bend in filthy wet conditions in Brazil to take fifth place and snatch his first championship from Ferrari by one point; 98 to Felipe Massa's 97. His drive at such a young age was remarkable in those conditions and put him amongst the few greats who had also mastered such dreadful conditions in astonishing drives. It was not to be his last. Nonetheless, Lewis would not take another championship until 2014.

McLaren failed to get the car into top condition for the 2009 season and Lewis knew he was not really in with a chance of the championship, though he still managed a fifth place, and the following year,

despite two collisions, he had shot up to 2nd place.

But the years that followed were to be Sebastian Vettel's glory years with Red Bull leaving Lewis, despite victories, unable to capitalise on his talents.

Understandably, Lewis had then had enough of being second fiddle, and in 2013 announced that he was leaving McLaren and joining Mercedes. Now the tables were about to be turned.

That first year was frustrating, the car not entirely balanced to his liking, for despite five pole positions there was only one victory, in Hungary.

But then, overcoming a series of car failures in 2014, Lewis took the title again and became almost unbeatable, winning again in 2015, 2017, 2018, 2019 and 2020; along the way, he became the driver with the most Grand Prix wins ever, reaching 103 at the end of the 2021 season.

DRIVING STYLE

Considered to be one of the most accomplished drivers on the grid, showing complete mastery of all areas of the sport. Lewis instinctively knows his car's limits and has garnered praise for his ability to adjust his drive in accordance. He pairs an inimitable ability to pressure the brakes hard so that there's no wastage or withholding in downforce yet no danger of locking the wheels either, with the skill to bring his car cleanly around a corner whilst on the very edge of instability without losing momentum. As far as the all-important concentration is concerned, Lewis's almost consistently faultless driving is now legendary, and he has been praised for his ability to maintain it throughout a race without losing mental or physical sharpness.

Lewis was incredibly fortunate to emerge alive from a crash with Max Verstappen in the 2021 Italian GP when the Dutch driver's car wheel struck Lewis in the head.

Lewis is one of a new generation of sports stars who use their fame to engage and attempt to rectify social injustices – Lewis's involvement in the Black Lives Matter Movement is of particular importance to him.

Lewis Hamilton is not only a powerful ambassador

for a sport that he loves, but he also employs his passion on matters of the environment, animal rights – he is a vegan – sustainable fashion and advocating for progress in the advancement of human rights. Equally, he wants to bring home the message to those who wish to follow in his footsteps that they should never "give up on their dreams". The Hamilton Commission, of which Lewis Hamilton is co-chair, was created to underline this message and also those of diversity, inclusivity and sustainability.

FORMULA ONE WORLD DRIVERS CHAMPIONSHIP: 2008, 2014, 2015, 2017, 2018, 2019, 2020 FORMULA ONE WORLD CONSTRUCTORS' CHAMPIONSHIP: 2014, 2015 2016, 2017, 2018, 2019, 2020, 2021 **DHL FASTEST LAP AWARD: 2014, 2015, 2017, 2019, 2020, 2021** FIA POLL TROPHY/ PIRELLI POLL POSITION AWARD: 2015, 2016, 2017, 2018, 2020 **HAWTHORNE MEMORIAL TROPHY: 2007, 2008, 2012, 2014, 2015, 2016, 2017, 2018, 2019, 2020, 2021** LORENZO BANDINI TROPHY 2009 **BREAKTHROUGH OF THE YEAR AWARD 2008** SPORTSMAN OF THE YEAR AWARD 2020 **BBC SPORTS PERSONALITY OF THE YEAR AWARD 2014, 2020** FIA PERSONALITY OF THE YEAR 2014, 2018, 2020, 2021 **MEMBER OF THE ORDER OF THE BRITISH EMPIRE** KNIGHT BACHELOR **HONORARY AWARD GRANADA**

Lewis Hamilton celebrates on the podium during the F1 Grand Prix of Spain at Circuit de Barcelona-Catalunya on May 09, 2021

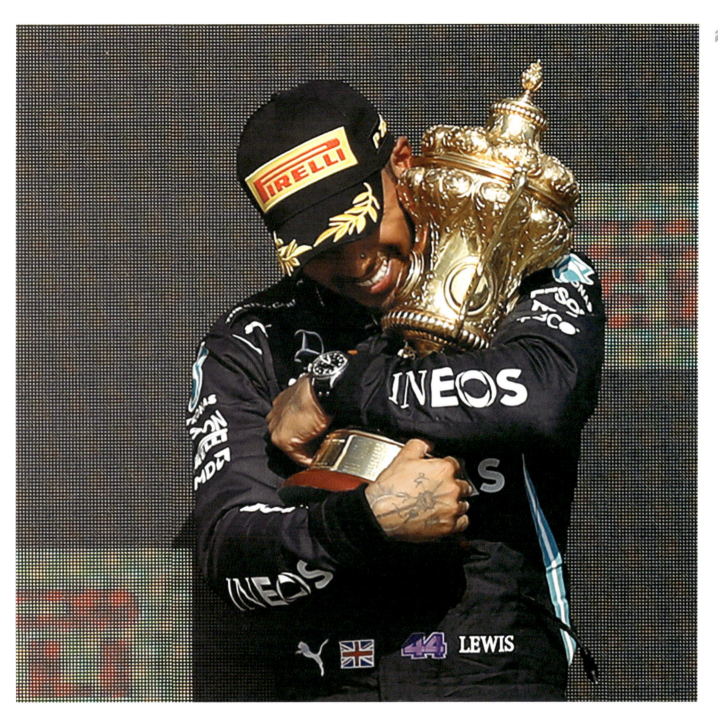

⌃ Lewis Hamilton holds the trophy on the podium after the Formula One British Grand Prix motor race at Silverstone motor racing circuit in Silverstone, England, July 18, 2021

⌐ Formula One World Drivers Champion Lewis Hamilton of Great Britain and Mercedes GP celebrates in parc ferme during the F1 Grand Prix of USA at Circuit of The Americas on November 03, 2019 in Austin, Texas

« Lewis Hamilton celebrates in parc ferme during the F1 Grand Prix of Bahrain at Bahrain International Circuit, March 28, 2021

SEBA
VETTEL

Sebastian Vettel was born in Heppenheim, Germany on the 3rd of July 1987.

Sebastian was only eight when he began racing karts in 1995 wanting to emulate his hero Michael Schumacher, and it was Schumacher's own mentor, Gerhard Noah, a track owner, who noticed the young Sebastian's talent. Noah helped Sebastian win karting titles, and before long, the young driver's potential was also brought to the attention of the Red Bull Junior Team, who took him on in 1998.

2001 saw him take the Junior Monaco Kart Cup, and by 2003 he was in open-wheel racing. Placing second in the overall standings in his first season of driving in the junior Formula BMW series, he claimed 18 victories from 20 races and won the championship in 2004 at the age of 17 gaining 387 points from a possible 400.

The next step was the Formula Three Euro Series in which he drove for ASL Mücke Motorsport in 2005 coming 5th in the 2005 Formula 3 Euro Series and earning himself the Rookie Cup with 63 points. That year, aged just 18, he was allowed to drive as a tester for Williams Formula One, and then tested for the BMW Sauber Formula One team.

In 2006, he came second in the Formula Three Euro Series. Neither did he escape injury; his finger was almost severed in a 170 mph crash at Spa-Francorchamps that year.

Coming one step closer to his dream, he was BMW Sauber's third driver in the 2006 Turkish Grand Prix and became the youngest, at 19 years and 53 days, and fastest driver to participate in a Grand Prix weekend in Turkey during a Friday free practice. He also set the fastest time at the Italian Grand Prix Friday practice sessions.

2007 was the year he finally broke into the big boys' club. Having been confirmed as test driver for BMW, a horrific crash involving Polish driver Robert Kubica in the Canadian Grand Prix – he escaped serious injury – put Sebastian in the seat for the United States Grand Prix at Indianapolis. Sebastian came home in 8th place but was displaced from the seat when Kubica returned for the following race.

When team Toro Rosso dropped Scott Speed, Sebastian was given the vacant seat for the remainder of the season – and promptly colliding with Red Bull teammate Mark Webber.

SEBASTIAN VETTEL RACE STATS

280 GRAND PRIX 53 WINS (18.92%) **3,061 POINTS** 3,499 LAPS LED **57 POLE POSITIONS** 38 FASTEST LAPS **122 PODIUMS** 8 HAT TRICKS **4 GRAND SLAMS** 41 RETIREMENTS **16,135 LAPS RACED** 77,506 KM RACED **16 SEASONS (2006-2021)** 9 TEAMMATES (ROBERT KUBICA, NICK HEIDFELD, VITANTO NIO LIUZZI, SÉBASTIEN BOURDAIS, MARK WEBBER, DANIEL RICCIARDO, KIMI RÄIKKÖNEN, CHARLES LECLERC, LANCE STROLL.)

In 2008 he finally made his breakthrough, retained by Toro Rosso for the 2008 season.

Yet despite the "racing prodigy" tag that was now being floated around his name, Vettel did not make a great impact on the F1 circuits, not managing higher than a 4th place in his first 21 races. He did, however, claim the youngest F1 race winner ever title with his first win at the Italian Grand Prix that year; he was just 21 years and 2 months of age. That win on a track drenched in rain and with a car that was below par showed his potential and impressed Red Bull sufficiently for them to recall him for their own team for the 2009 season. Vettel had finally understood how to handle the speed machine that was a Formula One car. "Baby Schumi" was born. A nickname, however, that Sebastian is not too happy with, preferring to create his own mythology than ride on the back of someone else's, which is exactly what he is doing on the track already.

So in 2009, Sebastian was in the seat vacated by David Coulthard, but his moment had not yet come for this was the year that Britain's Jenson Button took the top honours, beating Sebastian into 2nd place

with 95 points to 84.

But in 2010, the years of apprenticeship were over and he launched into four years of Grand Prix domination. His debut at the top of the podium was a strange affair, for he won just five races that season when he brought home his first F1 World Championship; he was only the third driver in F1 history to have won despite not being at the top of the driver's standings until the final race.

Sebastian decided early on to name all of his cars, and that memorable year his charges carried the venerable names of Luscious Liz and Randy Mandy. After Kinky Kylie in 2011, his other winners were Abbey, Hungry Heidi and Suzie, who rounded off the winning streak in 2013. On a roll, his car improving with every race as he told reporters later, he was the overwhelming presence in the 2011 season taking the top of the podium in 11 of the 19 races and even stronger in 2013 taking 13 victories home, equalling Michael Schumacher's haul from 2004.

Although his four-year unbeaten run was to come to

an abrupt end and years of drought would follow, he became the first F1 driver to win eight consecutive races and by the end of the year he had amassed a record nine straight wins.

As quickly as success had smiled on him she abandoned him and smiled on another favourite. In 2014, forced to retire in Australia, Monaco and Austria, he had the sad distinction of becoming the first reigning champion to fail to win a single race since Jacques Villeneuve, who achieved the same dubious honour in 1998.

It was time for a change of scenery even though his contract had one year still to run. Sebastian opted for Schumacher's old team, Scuderia Ferrari. For the German driver, "… the dream of a lifetime has come true."

Initially it seemed as though he was going to get back to the top swiftly after a victory in his second race in Malaysia and winning in Hungary; yet the fates were against him, and a 3rd place in the championship was all that he could manage in 2015 and a fourth in 2016.

DRIVING STYLE

Following his departure from Ferrari there were suggestions that he had never quite mastered the red cars and that leaving was a mental blow for him; but the driver himself denies that his is one of the most sensitive driving styles in Formula 1. He prefers a 'nervous' rear end, and writers have noted that in the corners he will 'rotate' the car around the inside front wheel and hit the throttle as fast as possible to prevent the rear from sliding. With Ferrari, this often resulted in a loss of grip mid-corner, and the instability left him open to attack from his competitors. Neither does he turn his head as much as other drivers in corners, looking upwards through the visor, thus preventing neck ache in long races.

His attention to his car's mechanical workings is paired with the ruthless streak that every winning driver must possess to some extent – evident in Vettel, for example, when he ignored his team's instruction to allow team Mate Webber – with whom team rivalry had turned to animosity – to win the Malaysian GP in 2013.

In 2017 and 2018, Sebastian returned to form to challenge Hamilton for the title but couldn't dislodge the dominant Brit, who was riding high and on course to equal Sebastian's four consecutive World Championships.

In 2019 and 2020, Vettel had fallen even further back, and the Ferrari dream had not only faded, with a 5th and then a 13th place at the end of the respective seasons, it was completely over. There was to be no following in Schumacher's footsteps; Sebastian was told that his contract would end with the 2020 season; a sad end to a boyhood dream.

The thought of retirement flitted across his mind, but he ignored its siren call and 2021 saw him with Aston Martin. But there, he found himself suddenly reduced to the middle of the table, whilst his erstwhile opponents raced far away from him. Sebastian remains optimistic for the new season, however, and is quoted as saying,

"The new rules offer a great opportunity in 2022, but we also have to remain realistic and not talk about being favourites, but look at how good our car is".

Sebastian's high level of concentration is wedded to his knowledge of the technical aspect of his cars. Behind the scenes he is always in consultation with his engineers. His visits to tyre factories provided him with insights into the tyres that could make or break his performances, where he asked as many questions as Michael Schumacher in the attempt to understand what his tyres and cars were capable of.

Away from racing, Sebastian and his childhood friend Hanna Prater have been married since 2019. They have two daughters and a baby son. Vettel senior also speaks English, French, Finnish and Italian – and avoids social media like the plague, the only Formula One driver in 2021 who has no social media presence.

F1 WORLD CHAMPIONSHIPS 2010, 2011, 2012, 2013 **ROOKIE OF THE YEAR, AUTOSPORT AWARDS 2008** LORENZO BANDINI TROPHY 2009, **BRITISH RACING DRIVER'S CLUB JOHNNY WAKEFIELD TROPHY 2009 (SETTING THE FASTEST RACE LAP OF THE SEASON ON THE SILVERSTONE GRAND PRIX CIRCUIT)** GERMAN SPORTS PERSONALITY OF THE YEAR 2010 **INTERNATIONAL RACING DRIVER CATEGORY AUTOSPORT AWARD 2010, 2011, 2012, 2013** GRANDS PRIX DE L'ACADEMIE DES SPORTS 2012, ("DOUBLE CONSECUTIVE FORMULA ONE WORLD CHAMPION AT THE AGE OF TWENTY FOUR — WINNER OF ELEVEN GRANDS PRIX OUT OF NINETEEN"). SILBERNES LORBEERBLATT 2012 IN RECOGNITION OF HIS WORLD TITLES AND HIS EXEMPLARY CHARACTER **AUTOSPORT MAGAZINE FORMULA ONE DRIVER OF THE YEAR IN 2009, 2011 AND 2013 IN A VOTE BY THE TEAM PRINCIPALS** DHL FASTEST LAP AWARD IN 2009, 2012 AND 2013 **EUROPEAN SPORTSPERSON OF THE YEAR BY THE INTERNATIONAL SPORTS PRESS ASSOCIATION IN 2010** POLISH PRESS AGENCY EUROPEAN SPORTSPERSON OF THE YEAR 2012 AND 2013 **BBC OVERSEAS SPORTS PERSONALITY OF THE YEAR 2013** LAUREUS WORLD SPORTS AWARDS SPORTSMAN OF THE YEAR 2014 **CONFARTIGIANATO MOTORI AWARD DRIVER OF THE YEAR 2015**

Sebastian Vettel of Germany and Ferrari drives during final practice for the Formula One Grand Prix of Austria at Red Bull Ring on June 20, 2015

MA

VERSTAPPE

Max Emilian Verstappen was born on the 30th of September 1997 in Hasselt, Belgium to father Jos, a former F1 racing driver, and mother Sophie Kumpen, who was a competitive kart driver. His parents are now separated.

He climbed into his kart at the age of four in Limburg, Belgium, and because of his karting spent more time with his father, meaning that most of his life took place in Holland where his friends were, and he eventually took Dutch nationality at the the age of 18. It was in Limburg that he competed in the Mini Junior Championship, and began to accumulate victories.

Often skipping classes with his dad's support, he competed in the Mini Junior Championship of his home province gravitating to the Rotax Max Minimax class in 2006, taking the honours in the Belgian Championship winning again in 2007, at the Dutch Minimax Championship

He continued his winning ways when he joined Team Pex Racing, a CRG customer team, in 2009, the same year that he was victorious in the Flemish Minimax and Belgian KF5 championships.

As his winning ways continued, it was obvious that he was going to go far.

In 2011, Following the WSK Euro Series victory in 2011, 2012, saw Max take the WSK Master Series in the KF2 class and the KF2 class South Garda Winter Cup. On the heels of a that less successful 2012 season, he returned in 2013 to win the European KF and KZ championships. He was 15, when he took the 2013 World KZ championship.

MAX VERSTAPPEN RACE STATS

141 GRAND PRIX 20 WINS (14.18%) **1,557.50 POINTS** 1,603 LAPS LED **13 POLE POSITIONS** 16 FASTEST LAPS **60 PODIUMS** 3 HAT TRICKS **1 GRAND SLAMS** 29 RETIREMENTS **8,162 LAPS RACED** 36,891 KM RACED **8 SEASONS (2006–2021)** 7 TEAMMATES (DANIIL KVYAT, JEAN-ÉRIC VERGNE, CARLOS SAINZ, DANIEL RICCIARDO, PIERRE GASLY, ALEXANDER ALBON, SERGIO PÉREZ.)

2013 was an exciting year for the young driver, for that year he sat behind the wheel of a Formula Renault car and tested several other Formula 2 Renaults and F3 cars. He clocked up faster Formula Renault times than vets such as Eddie Cheever III. It was time for a step up, which he took the next year with his maiden race in the FIA European Formula 3 Championship, ending the season in 3rd place.

He was not destined to stay third for long.

That same year, he joined the Red Bull Junior Team, talented enough to leap from F3 to F1, taking part in the free practice for the Japanese Grand Prix, making him the youngest driver to participate in a Grand Prix weekend. And he broke another record by entering the 2015 Australian Grand Prix aged 17 years and 166 days.

DRIVING STYLE

Criticised for overly aggressive driving which has caused collisions, clipping other cars and aggressive blocking, he was summoned for a lecture from F1's director Charlie Whiting, with other drivers warning that he was going to cause a major accident if he did not change his tactics.

Max is quoted as saying, "If you just say 'this is my driving style', this is how it's going to be, you will not be quick. I think you learn in your whole racing career from go-karting to F3 to whatever, every weekend the car behaves a bit differently. So, you always have to adjust to it."

Relying on his intuition, Max, though inexperienced, can rely on his relentless preparation, which will help him to master a nervous rear end or negotiate flooded tracks, and his ability to instantly assess a situation can get him out of trouble. He's also more mature, aware now that he doesn't need to take the risks he used to take that endangered other drivers, an attitude that has borne fruit, as with his maturity and the right car has come his first World Championship.

Max gained his first points at Malaysia making him the youngest driver to score World Championship points, at 17 years 188 days. This was a young man in a hurry, and the Toro Rosso team had been glad to hire him in 2014. His potential was abundantly clear when he was awarded Rookie of the Year, Personality of the Year and Action of the Year (at the Blanchimont corner in the Belgian Grand Prix he had overtaken Felipe Nasr on the outside) titles.

Whilst still awaiting his first championship title, Max has been pressing hard and making the veteran stars of the track look nervously in their mirrors.

Having taken his first victory in 2016, he followed with a 6th place in 2017, 4th place in 2018, 3rd in 2019 and 2020. In 2021, he finally achieved the dream with his first GP World Championship victory, secured in the final race of the season at Abu Dhabi gaining 395.50 points for the season just ahead of Lewis Hamilton's 387.50.

MAX VERSTAPPEN HONOURS INCLUDE

F1 WORLD CHAMPIONSHIP 2021 **AUTOSPORT AWARDS ROOKIE OF THE YEAR 2015** FIA ACTION OF THE YEAR AWARD 2014, 2015, 2016, 2019 **FIA PERSONALITY OF THE YEAR 2015, 2016, 2017** YOUNGEST DRIVER TO COMPETE IN FORMULA 1: 2015 AUSTRALIAN GRAND PRIX (17 YEARS, 166 DAYS) **YOUNGEST DRIVER WITH FASTEST LAP: 2016 BRAZILIAN GRAND PRIX (19 YEARS AND 44 DAYS)** YOUNGEST DRIVER TO SCORE POINTS IN FORMULA 1: 2015 MALAYSIAN GRAND PRIX (17 YEARS 180 DAYS) **YOUNGEST DRIVER TO FINISH ON THE PODIUM/WIN AN F1 RACE: 2016 SPANISH GRAND PRIX (18 YEARS 228 DAYS)** MOST PODIUM FINISHES IN A SEASON: 22 IN 2021 **YOUNGEST DRIVER TO SCORE A GRAND SLAM: 23 YEARS 277 DAYS AT THE AUSTRIAN GRAND PRIX ON THE 4TH OF JULY 2021**

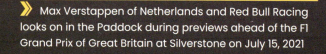

Max Verstappen of Netherlands and Red Bull Racing looks on in the Paddock during previews ahead of the F1 Grand Prix of Great Britain at Silverstone on July 15, 2021

DAN
RICCIARD

Daniel was born in Perth, Western Australia on the 1st of July 1989 to his father Giuseppe and mother Grace, an Australian of Italian parentage. His father had moved to Australia from Sicily in Italy. As a young boy, Daniel watched his father racing at the Barbagallo Raceway 50 km north of Perth.

Daniel's father, known to all as "Joe", worked hard to support his son, who began karting quite late in comparison to other F1 drivers; he was nine years old, and despite driving a Van Dieman car that was 15 years old, he finished eighth in the 2005 Western Australia Formula Ford championship.

Nonetheless, it was obvious that Daniel had talent, and he won a scholarship with Eurasia Motorsport for the Formula BMW Asia championship. That season, Daniel finished in 3rd position with two victories under his belt and a pole position. In the Formula BMW World Final he took 5th position with Fortec Motorsport.

But Daniel decided that in order to move up the F1 ladder, he needed to be in Europe, where, in 2007 he joined RP Motorsport in Formula Renault, where he stayed for a second season. He was rewarded with his first title, in the Western European Cup, only missing out on the Eurocup to Valtteri Bottas.

Daniel's first taste of F3 came in the 2008 season at the Nürburgring in the Formula 3 Euro, driving for the SG Formula team, and by 2009 – the year of his F1 track debut when he tested for Red Bull Racing in the young drivers test at Circuito de Jerez in December – he'd moved to Carlin Motorsport for the British Formula 3 Championship. Following an outing with Tech 1 Racing Portugal, he came back with a vengeance to take the British F3 Championship, the first Australian to do so since David Brabham in 1989, also driving in the rookie test for Red Bull.

Tech 1 Racing were impressed enough to hire him for the 2010 season. It proved to be an eventful one with punishment for hindering other drivers, a barrel roll at Silverstone and six poles in 12 races. In the Formula Renault 3.5 series, his skill was apparent when he finished just two points behind Mikhail Aleshin, the reigning champion, despite his car flipping over at Silverstone, and he was still in Renault 3.5 in 2011 when he took a seat for the Friday practice sessions for Red Bull's sister team Toro Rosso after an impressive performance representing Red Bull Racing at the young drivers test at the Yas Marina Circuit in November 2010 (his fastest lap was 1.3 seconds faster than World Champion Sebastian Vettel). This was the year his career took off, for in June he was offered

the seat with HRT for the British Grand Prix as a replacement for Narain Karthikeyan at Red Bull.

Even though the car was nestled at the back of the grid in Abu Dhabi and Brazil and Daniel hadn't been able to set the track on fire that season, his results were good enough to warrant a permanent seat with Toro Rosso in 2012, driving a car powered by Ferrari and racing for them again in 2013.

DANIEL RICCIARDO RACE STATS

210 GRAND PRIX 8 WINS (3.80%) **1,274 POINTS** 340 LAPS LED **3 POLE POSITIONS** 16 FASTEST LAPS **32 PODIUMS** 34 RETIREMENTS **12,332 LAPS RACED** 58,274 KM RACED **11 SEASONS (2011-2021)** 12 TEAMMATES (JAMIE ALGUERSUARI, SEBASTIEN BUEMI, VITANTONIO LIUZZI, NARAIN KARTHIKEYAN, JAN CHAROUZ, JEAN-ÉRIC VERGNE, DANIIL KVYAT, SEBASTIAN VETTEL, MAX VERSTAPPEN, NICO HÜLKENBERG, ESTABAN OCON, LANDO NORRIS.)

When Mark Webber retired, Daniel took over the vacant seat alongside Vettel at Red Bull for 2014. He repaid the confidence with exciting runs giving him a 3rd place finish at the end of the season after wins in Canada, Hungary and Belgium and placing 3rd in Spain, Monaco, Britain, Singapore and the USA. He pulled in another 3rd place in 2016 ahead of Verstappen and Vettel. Ricciardo swapped to Renault for the 2019 and 2020 seasons and although 2020 produced poorer results than for most of his more recent outings when he'd been nipping at the heels of the leaders, he still managed a 5th place.

Deciding it was time for a change of seat, Daniel swapped to McLaren for the 2021 season and took the wheel of a Mercedes MCL35M with his teammate, up-and-coming star Lando Norris. Unfortunately, the results have been less than he would have hoped, until the 2021 Italian Grand Prix where McLaren took the only 1-2 of the season, with Ricciardo notching his first win with the team.' But he still fights for every place and when Daniel is behind him, then no driver is safe from being passed. McLaren have retained his services for the 2022 season.

DRIVING STYLE

The "Honey Badger", a nickname that Ricciardo has trailed in his wake for many years now whenever his racing style is under consideration, refers to that animal being "the most fearless animal in the animal kingdom. When you look at it, he seems quite cute and cuddly, but as soon as someone crosses his territory .... he turns into a bit of a savage and he'll go after anything".

Ricciardo is admired for his superb race craft that will enable him to survive extraordinary passing moves. His ability to read a race, however, puts him on the same level as greats such as Lewis Hamilton or Fernando Alonso. Unlike Hamilton, his tyres undergo less punishment and last longer, blistering speeds notwithstanding. He has the driving abilities of a world champion – but without the fickle Lady Luck in your crew, that honour has, as yet, proven an elusive goal.

DANIEL RICCIARDO HONOURS INCLUDE

BRDC THE BRUCE MCLAREN TROPHY 2013 TROFEO LORENZO BANDINI 2014 **CONFARTIGIANATO MOTORI DRIVER OF THE YEAR 2014** GQ AUSTRALIA SPORTSMAN OF THE YEAR 2014 **BRDC THE BRUCE MCLAREN TROPHY 2014** BRDC THE INNES IRELAND TROPHY 2014 **BRDC THE INNES IRELAND TROPHY 2015** LAUREUS WORLD SPORTS AWARD FOR BREAKTHROUGH PERFORMANCE OF THE YEAR 2015 **BRDC THE BRUCE MCLAREN TROPHY 2016** CONFARTIGIANATO MOTORI DRIVER OF THE YEAR 2018

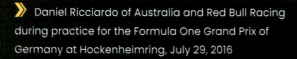

Daniel Ricciardo of Australia and Red Bull Racing during practice for the Formula One Grand Prix of Germany at Hockenheimring, July 29, 2016

⌃ Daniel Ricciardo of Australia driving the McLaren F1 Team MCL35M Mercedes makes a pitstop during the Grand Prix of Monaco at Circuit de Monaco on May 23, 2021

« Daniel Ricciardo of Australia and Red Bull Racing during the Monaco Formula One Grand Prix at Circuit de Monaco on May 27, 2018

« Daniel Ricciardo driving the McLaren F1 Team MCL35M Mercedes on track during qualifying for the F1 Grand Prix of Monaco at Circuit de Monaco on May 22, 2021

⌐ Daniel Ricciardo driving the McLaren F1 Team MCL35M Mercedes on track during final practice ahead of the F1 Grand Prix of Monaco at Circuit de Monaco on May 22, 2021

SER
PÉREZ

Born Sergio Michel Pérez Mendoza in Guadalajara, Mexico on January the 26th 1990 to Antonio and his mother Marilú, the man with the nickname of "Checo" now sits behind the wheel of a Red Bull Racing Honda RB16B having moved across from Racing Point RP20 in 2021 where he had spent two seasons in the Mercedes.

Sergio was already racing karts in 1996 at the age of 6, encouraged by his father, who had been a stock car racer. It was clear that Sergio possessed an exceptional talent when he won four races in his first year and finished second. In the Youth Class, he was the youngest entrant ever to take part, earning a 4th place, and ended the following year with even better results in the junior category winning the championship, the youngest driver ever to do so.

He continued to enter competitions as the youngest driver and draw attention to himself to the extent that in 2000 he was singled out by the scouts for Escuderia Telemex.

Withdrawals from the two Shifter Championships, the 80cc and the 125cc dented his hopes at the point where he was leading in both categories, but he continued to impress, and by 2005, Sergio took on the challenge of moving to Europe and the German Formula BMW ADAC series. After a brief outing in the A1 Grand Prix 2006-07 season, he moved to Oxford in the UK, and in 2008 began driving in the 2008-09 Asia Series for the Campos Grand Prix team. Not since 1990 had a Mexican been involved in racing at this level (Giovanni Aloi). Sergio won his first two GP2 races back to back.

Sauber were the next team to place their fate in his hands; finally he had made it to Formula One, only the fifth Mexican to do so. It was 2010, the year he joined the Ferrari Driver Academy; he would take over from Nick Heidfeld at Sauber in 2011.

SERGIO PÉREZ RACE STATS

217 GRAND PRIX 2 WINS (0.92%) **896 POINTS** 108 LAPS LED **6 FASTEST LAPS** 15 PODIUMS **28 RETIREMENTS** 12,612 LAPS RACED **59,905 KM RACED** 11 SEASONS (2011-2021) **12 TEAMMATES (KAMUI KOBAYASHI, PEDRO DE LA ROSA, ESTEBAN GUTIERREZ, JENSON BUTTON, NICO HÜLKENBERG, DANIEL JUNCADELLA, ALFONSO CELIS, ESTEBAN OCON, GEORGE RUSSELL, NICHOLAS LATIFI, LANCE STROLL, MAX VERSTAPPEN.)**

It was not the start in F1 he would have wanted. Upon exiting the tunnel in the third part of qualifying, he swayed to the right and struck the barrier, slid back across the chicane and slammed into the TecPro barrier separating the track from the escape road, which had been improved following a similar accident. Qualifying was suspended for more than half an hour, whilst a medical team extricated Sergio from the car and repairs were carried out on the barrier. Sergio was fortunate in that he suffered 'only' from concussion and a sprained thigh, though he wasn't able to participate in the race the next day.

So a disappointing first season with a 16th place finish, but Sauber kept the faith for the 2012 season. He finished a respectable 10th.

Change, however, was what he needed and he replaced Lewis Hamilton at McLaren for 2013. This proved to be an unfortunate but fortunately short-lived love affair, with teammate Jenson Button at one point only just stopping short of accusing Sergio of dangerous driving. Sergio eventually came home in 11th place that season behind Button in 9th.

From then on, Sergio raced for the Force India Team until 2019. His form improved, and he then brought his car in 10th, 9th, 7th, 7th and finally 8th in 2018 – a difficult year that had brought a mediocre performance in Singapore, then two collisions, and a brake failure that forced him to retire in his homeland race in Mexico. On top of that, the Force India Team was put into administration, but fortunately rescued by a consortium which started up the team again as Racing Point Force India. The team became simply, Racing Point, for 2019. Sergio would stay for another season.

It seemed that history might repeat itself, however, although he overcame car difficulties and a crash to bring in points and work his way to a final 10th place.

DRIVING STYLE

The media even call him F1's most underrated driver (he's reported to have been amongst the 10 front cars per lap in 2019 for 43% of the time, which gave him the best results amongst the midfield drivers). Although accused of being an "extreme" driver, a word that seems to mean different things to different people, his understanding of tyre management has earned him a reputation as a first-rate expert, able to extract the most from his rubbers.

Whilst he was once thought of as using a "strange driving style – which worked very well for some circuits", according to Jenson Button, who, when they were teammates, also felt that Sergio "has to calm down" – the Mexican is very fast, is not one to give in and has grown in confidence in his qualities and ability to assess the big picture, as his results prove. Valued, also, for his consistency in dealing with whatever he is faced with on the track and his record of making few mistakes, these character traits when paired with his ability to make his car use fuel as judiciously as possible make Sergio a valued driver for any team.

From 2020, he at last began to bring in the results of which he was capable, gaining his first top spot on the podium, at the Sakhir GP (the first win for a Mexican driver – since Pedro Rodríguez – in 50 years) after a 2nd place in Turkey. And he did so even though he had again been plagued with engine trouble that season, been struck from behind (returning, incredibly, to win the race) and incurred penalties on two occasions. Oh yes, and had been struck down with the Covid virus!

There were, therefore, good reasons for Red Bull Honda to use Sergio when his Racing Point contract was not renewed and have him partner Max Verstappen in 2021.

The change for Sergio was telling, as were the results, for despite another penalty and a smash-up in Hungary, he brought home another win, two 4th and two 5th place finishes, which put him on 4th place at the end of the season – showing that given the chance and the car, he is able to challenge at the highest level.

A Roman Catholic, in November 2012, Pérez unveiled the Checo Pérez Foundation, which supports orphans and children with cancer. Paola, Sergio's sister, was the foundation's president.

Sergio Pérez is married to Carola Martínez, with whom he has two children.

VALT

BOTTAS

V altteri Viktor Bottas, born on the 28th of August in Nastola, Finland in 1989, has been making life uncomfortable for the F1 world champions for many years now, threatening in his Mercedes, as he did in 2019 when he was 2nd in the World Championship, to make them pay for any mistakes they make. If any driver looked in his mirror in recent years, the chances were that Valtteri would be the man worrying you. In 2019, for example, Valtteri qualified second fastest behind Lewis Hamilton, overtaking Lewis in the race and holding the first position with spectacular driving. Besides that, he recorded the fastest lap of the race. He is not a man to underestimate.

Father Rauno and mother Marianne watched their son take the wheel of his karts at an early age, so that by the age of 6 he was racing in the snow of Finland. His talent was apparent at that early stage when he was placed 8th in the 2005 Karting World Cup for the P.D.B Racing Team. Even though he was ineligible – lacking the relevant licence – he showed his potential by competing in and winning three of the four races in the Formula Renault UK Winter Series, but he did go on to win the Formula Renault Eurocup and the Formula Renault Northern European Cup both in 2008.

One year later, he was accepted by championship team ART Grand Prix for the Formula Three Euroseries; with two poles but no victories he still managed third place, but drove superbly in the Masters of Formula 3 event that same year to win the competition, setting the fastest lap on the way to doing so. He topped that by claiming the title again the following year, 2010. That made him the first driver ever to win the masters title twice.

This success brought him to the attention of the Williams Formula One team and he was hired as a test driver. It was during this period that he added the GP3 Series title to his collection, driving to victory in the final four races.

Valtteri did not have long to wait before the longed-for call came: in 2013 he was going to partner Pastor Maldonado in the Williams-Renault for the F1 2013 season. He scored his first points at the United States Grand Prix with an 8th position, and despite the year proving difficult, he finished ahead of his teammate in the driver standings. Just as well, for Maldonado was then replaced by Felipe Massa.

VALTTERI BOTTAS RACE STATS

179 GRAND PRIX 10 WINS (5.58%) **20 POLE POSITIONS** 1,738 POINTS **841 LAPS LED** 19 FASTEST LAPS **67 PODIUMS** 2 HAT TRICKS **17 RETIREMENTS** 10,910 LAPS RACED **51,349 KM RACED** 10 SEASONS (2012-2021) **7 TEAMMATES (BRUNO SENNA, PASTOR MALDONADO, FELIPE MASSA, FELIPE NASR, SUSIE WOLFF, LEWIS HAMILTON, GEORGE RUSSELL.)**

A new Williams' deal with Mercedes improved the car's performance and Valtteri took full advantage in 2014 in Austria, standing on the podium for the first time. He took five more podiums, storming from 14th on the grid to a second-place finish at the British GP to claim his second consecutive career podium and place the William's flag on 4th place at the end of the season.

Reason enough to keep the Fin at Williams for 2015. But Valtteri hurt his back, and despite two podiums, he was struck by Räikkönen in Russia and ended the year in 5th place. He would have to be content with a disappointing year in 2016, just one podium, in Canada, although he did achieve an unofficial Formula One speed record at the Baku City Circuit in qualifying: 378 km/h or 235 mph. Valtteri was 8th by the end of that season.

Having raced for Williams since 2013, Valtteri now opted to take the seat at Mercedes for the 2017 season. His performance must have worried both his new partner at Mercedes, Hamilton, and their rival Vettel, for Valtteri drove a season to

remember. It was a year he would gain pole over Lewis at Bahrain and fight back to a 6th place despite spinning into 12th behind the safety car in China.

In Russia in April, he was finally rewarded with his first GP win, taking on both Vettel and Räikkönen's Ferraris from third on the grid, the fifth Fin to stand as a winner on the podium. It was an exciting season all round for Valtteri, involving two collisions with Räikkönen, a retirement and a superb catch-up race to take 2nd in Canada. At one point he was just 15 points behind Hamilton in the table. Four poles and three wins later, he was 3rd at the season's end just 12 points behind Vettel in 2nd place.

Slipping to 5th in 2018, with the dubious honour of being only the second Mercedes driver to finish a season without a win (mind you, the other driver was Michael Schumacher in 2012! – good company), Mercedes kept the faith with him, and he powered back with his best performance to date in 2019, well clear of Verstappen, to claim

2nd place with 326 points, behind a dominant Lewis Hamilton's 413. And this despite a crash in Mexico during qualifying and engine failure in Brazil. Mercedes claimed several one-two finishes, whilst Valtteri had four wins, fifteen podiums, five poles and three fastest laps to his credit.

Nonetheless, Valtteri decided on just a one-year extension through 2020 with Mercedes. It was to prove a year of mixed fortunes, involving tyre failures, pole positions, retirements in Italy and at the Nürburgring, starts from second on the grid, strikes by flying debris, spinning six times in one race, and missed chances. But with the indomitable spirit that had brought him in 2nd in 2019, he claimed his second successive 2nd place for the 2020 season, too.

Having decided on another contract extension through 2021, once again, it was not an easy season for Valtteri with tyre wear and sensor issues taking their toll on his position in the table. On one infamous day (Monaco) the crew failed to get his tyre off in the pit and put an end to his race on the 31st lap.

DRIVING STYLE

Just a few years ago, Valtteri analysed his weak points and vowed to rectify them, mentioning that: "It looks as though my driving style does not fit so well with what the car needs". The ensuing results proved that he was a man of his word. Continuing to work on his technique, Valtteri said of himself that he was really confident, mentally, and in a good place.

Valtteri is famous for staying cool under pressure which helps him stay composed while driving. He has rightly earned a place amongst the top drivers on the grid. Given the right circumstances, he can beat anyone on the circuit for speed, and the mistakes he does make are rare beasts and seldom produce dramatic results. His prudent style has not been without criticism, however; for example, he was excoriated for his "safe, risk-free driving style" in Bahrain for not attempting to pass Vettel, despite his superior speed in the final stage of the race. Notwithstanding, and even though he has predicted that with Alfa Romeo in 2022, "I can't expect us to win races next year", he will now be a free man, the number 1 driver at Alfa Romeo, freed from the straight-jacket as the Mercedes' no 2.

Whatever happens, Valtteri's achievements to date will make him one of the best drivers ever to emerge from the Scandinavian country.

When asked about his teammate, Lewis Hamilton was fulsome in his praise: "We've motivated one another to keep pushing through the ups and the downs. He has been the best teammate I've had the pleasure of working with." Hamilton also mentioned that Valtteri's speed and resilience has been impressive adding, "where you truly stand out to me is the human being you are".

The Finn has proven a faithful driver to his teams, but his fifth season with Mercedes was to be his last. Despite coming home 3rd at the season's end, he announced that from 2022, he would be steering for another famous marque: Alfa Romeo F1. The instability of the past at Mercedes, the recurring worry about whether his contract would be renewed would be over, and Valtteri has expressed his relief that the new multi-year contract will free him from that pressure at least. The move will mean that Valtteri and Alfa Romeo team principal Fred Vasseur will be reunited, having worked together at ART in F3 in 2009, 2010, and in GP3 in 2011. Alfa will be just the third F1 team after Williams and Mercedes that Valtteri will have driven for. That kind of loyalty is good for teams and drivers hoping to improve and challenge for the big races, and Alfa Romeo and Valtteri Bottas are certainly up for the fight.

Valtteri expressed his excitement to the media about the move: "A new chapter in my racing career is opening ... a new challenge with an iconic manufacturer ... it's going to be an honour to represent this marque... and I am relishing the opportunity to help lead the team forward up the grid". And he left no doubt that Verstappen, Hamilton and co. will still need to use those rear view mirrors carefully and take heed of the Flying Finn!

VALTTERI BOTTAS HONOURS INCLUDE

SKY SPORTS AWARD FOR MOST IMPROVED DRIVER 2014 CONFARTIGIANATO MOTORI DRIVER OF THE YEAR 2017 LORENZO BANDINI TROPHY 2018 DHL FASTEST LAP AWARD 2018 AKK-MOTORSPORT DRIVER OF THE YEAR 2019

>> Valtteri Bottas driving the Mercedes AMG Petronas F1 Team Mercedes W10 on track during practice for the F1 Grand Prix of Azerbaijan at Baku City Circuit on April 26, 2019

CHA
LECLERC

Charles Marc Hervé Perceval Leclerc was born in Monte Carlo, Monaco, on the 16th of October 1997 to his father Hervé and mother Pascale. His father died in 2017, just before Charles took victory in the Formula 2 Baku round that year. Hervé Leclerc had driven in Formula 3 competitions during the 1980s and 1990s.

Charle's remarkable career began in 2005 when his talent was on display in the French PACA Championship; he took the title in 2005, 2006 and 2008.

By the following year, it was plain that here was a young man with a fast future; the French Cadet Championship was his that year, and in 2010 he won again, this time in the Junior Monaco Kart Cup in the KF3 class. That success continued into 2011 with victories in the CIK-FIA KF3 World Cup, the CIK-FIA Karting Academy Trophy and the ERDF Junior Kart Masters.

His potential now clear, in 2012 he was with the ART Grand Prix team, as he moved up into the KF2 category. Their faith was rewarded when he won the WSK Euro Series title. In the CIK-FIA European KF2 Championship and the CIK-FIA Under 18 World Karting Championship he came home 2nd in both competitions. Taking another victory in the South Garda Winter Cup in 2013 during his final year of karting, he was also runner-up in the CIK-FIA World KZ Championship. Max Verstappen took the full honours.

Then came the time for the real testing of his skills; he was hired by British team Fortec Motorsports for the Formula Renault 2.0 Alps Championship. 7 podiums brought him home as runner-up. He added three more podiums during the Eurocup Formula Renault 2.0 competition.

With the Dutch team Van Amersfoort Racing he took his first laps in Formula 3 in the FIA Formula 3 European Championship. Three wins saw him take the lead in the table only to be finally thwarted, thanks to a collision with Lance Stroll, and finish 4th. ART Gand Prix and Arden International were eager to bring the young driver back into the fold, and ART signed him up for 2016.

By the time he took pole position for the race in Bahrain in 2017, he was in the Formula 2 series racing for the Italian Prema Racing team, who have strong links with Ferrari.

If there were any doubts about where this young man was heading they were dispelled during this season. Showing superb tenacity in adversity from collisions, penalties, overheating tyres and team mistakes, nonetheless, he came out victorious in the FIA Formula 2 Championship in his rookie season in the main F1 feeder series. It was an astonishing fight back making Charles, at 19 years 356 days old, the youngest ever champion of the main support series for Formula 1. Nico Hülkenberg had been the last driver to accomplish the feat, in 2009, and Charles thus joined Nico Rosenberg and Lewis Hamilton in that elite club.

CHARLES LECLERC RACE STATS

81 GRAND PRIX 2 WINS (2.5%) **9 POLE POSITIONS** 560 POINTS **306 LAPS LED** 4 FASTEST LAPS **13 PODIUMS** 14 RETIREMENTS **4,896 LAPS RACED** 21,396 KM RACED **6 SEASONS (2016-2021)** (2 SEASONS NON-COMPETING) **7 TEAMMATES (ESTEBAN GUTIERREZ, ROMAIN GROSJEAN, PASCAL WEHRLEIN, MARCUS ERICSSON, ANTONIO GIOVINAZZI, SEBASTIAN VETTEL, CARLOS SAINZ.)**

Charles had gained F1 racing experience when he'd joined the Ferrari Driver Academy and driven as a development driver for Haas F1 Team and Scuderia Ferrari. His performance in the test after the Hungarian Grand Prix when he drove a Ferrari SF70H impressed everyone, as he was fastest on the first test day.

Charles's magic year arrived in 2018. The Alfa Romeo Sauber F1 team signed him to replace Pascal Wehrlein, a momentous event, as no driver from Monaco had appeared in F1 since 1994 and the era of Olivier Beretta.

So Charles started off in the 2018 Formula One World

Championship, taking his first points by coming in 6th in the fourth race in Azerbaijan. It was a season not without its problems; two collisions, one after his brakes failed, a loose wheel and a pile-up that saw Fernando Alonso catapulted over Charles's head. Oh yes, and suspension damage. 6th was the best placing he would achieve. But as the season progressed, the improvements became visible and Charles pulled in four finishes in 7th, all in the last 6 races, three of them in the final three outings of the season.

It was now obvious to Scuderia Ferrari that this young man was a potential champion, and they signed him up for 2019. It was a terrific season, which, although he didn't win the championship, brought him ten podium finishes, four fastest laps and the most pole positions that season, two wins and two runner-up placings. He was up amongst the big boys at the end of the season in 4th place, just ahead of Vettel, and only 14 points shy of Verstappen in 3rd.

He could be proud to be the first non-Mercedes driver to win the Pole Position Award.

DRIVING STYLE

Charles once said of his style of driving: "I've been struggling more and have more tyre degradation compared to Seb. (Sebastian Vettel) … maybe I'm driving a bit too aggressively now in races".

Tearing into every corner, he has discovered, takes its toll on the tyres, and this in turn eventually slows him down. His aggressive style makes some tracks, like the Hungaroring, which has many twists and turns, somewhat of a challenge for the young driver; they demand earlier braking and that drivers hold the braking for longer, so technique is paramount in such situations. Charles admits to struggling more than his competitors do when confronted with such conditions. Charles's ideal car will be one that demands less from the tyres, enabling him to put the car through more stress in the battle for speed.

2020 was disappointing, therefore, in comparison with his Ferrari debut. A collision, an accident, crashing out in Italy, damage and electrics all combined at various stages to thwart his ambitions after a promising runner-up position in his first outing in Austria. After that, he was never closer than third, with two 4th place finishes. It was a somewhat meagre tally of 98 points as the season closed.

Charles's contract runs now until 2024, so the team's confidence has not been dented. His teammate for the year 2021 was Carlos Sainz Jr. It was to be another season of mishaps, though, for although he showed that he could take on the veterans – he gained pole in Monaco but was unable to start the race, and pole in Azerbaijan

– Hamilton ultimately proved too strong a rival, despite the British driver's collision with Verstappen. Charles took his first podium of the year in second place, however. He was still only managing 4th at best by the time the Italian GP had finished, leaving him well adrift of the leaders with 104 points to table leader Verstappen's 226.50. He ended the season in 7th place with 159 points, just one point behind another young shooting star, Lando Norris. Leclerc's race to dethrone the F1 beasts such as Lewis Hamilton promises to be a thrilling one.

Charles Leclerc's current girlfriend is Charlotte Sine, daughter of a Monegasque entrepreneur. Leclerc is also multilingual, speaking Italian and English besides his native French.

CHARLES LECLERC HONOURS INCLUDE

AUTOSPORT AWARDS ROOKIE OF THE YEAR, 2017 FIA ROOKIE OF THE YEAR, 2017 AUTOSPORT AWARDS ROOKIE OF THE YEAR, 2018 FIA ROOKIE OF THE YEAR, 2018 CONFARTIGIANATO MOTORI BEST YOUNG DRIVER, 2018 MONACO MEDAL OF HONOUR, 2020

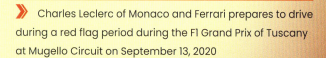

Charles Leclerc of Monaco and Ferrari prepares to drive during a red flag period during the F1 Grand Prix of Tuscany at Mugello Circuit on September 13, 2020

#essereFerrari

LAN

NORRIS

L ando Norris is one of the young stars of the sport. He was born in Bristol, England, on the 13th of November 1999 to father Adam and mother Cisca, who is Belgian. Oliver, his older brother, was also a kart driver at a competitive level.

Lando went to the Millfield School in the town of Street in Somerset in Southern England, and as his interest in academic achievement was not very pronounced, he was later given a full-time personal tutor with whom he studied physics and mathematics.

Initially interested in motorcycle racing, a visit to the local kart track with his father changed his mind, and he often could be seen with his father as a spectator at the championships. The family decamped to Glastonbury, where Lando became a day pupil at school, to help further his racing career. He was soon competing with brother Oliver.

By the age of 7, he was ready to race in competitions, showing his determination by taking pole position.

Karting remained the main focus of his life until 2014; he competed in KF-Junior karting. His winning streak began with the CIK FIA European Championship, which he won, and continued with the International Super Cup. These were followed by victory in the WSK Euro Series. As a protégé of Ricky Flynn Motorsport in 2014, he became the youngest karting World Champion, adding the CIK-FIA KF World Championship to his winning tally.

Thus ended his karting career as he entered the world of car racing in the Ginette Junior Championships, again showing his potential by taking the Rookie Cup having won four races and finishing in 3rd place.

Carlin Motorsport took him on for the 2015 season in the MSA Formula Championship, which has since been renamed the F4 British Championship. He clocked up fourteen podiums in total claiming eight victories and also drove for Mücke Motorsport in the Italian and ADAC Formula 4 championships, again raking in another six podiums.

For 2016, Lando bounced around between the Toyota Racing series, taking home 6 victories with the M2 competition team, a highly successful Formula Renault 2.0 season in the Eurocup, and the Northern European Cup, both of which series he won, and winning four of the eleven races in the BRDC British Formula 3 Championship.

With Carlin Motorsport, he then started out into the 2017 season in the European Formula 3 Championship. It was to

prove an-eye-catching season, for with twenty podiums in thirty races he secured nine victories and thus the title.

With five championships in four years, he could not fail to have caught the eye of the big F1 teams; it was the McLaren team that took the bait first. They had taken him on as a junior in 2017, and he finished the second fastest lap in testing at the Hungaroring, gaining himself a permanent spot as McLaren test and reserve driver for 2018. He took part in more practice sessions that year and was unlucky to have to retire from two races in the 2018 FIA Formula 2 Championship but still managed to be 2nd at the end of the season.

LANDO NORRIS RACE STATS

60 GRAND PRIX 306 POINTS **1 POLE POSITION** 31 LAPS LED **3 FASTEST LAPS** 5 PODIUMS **8 RETIREMENTS** 4,225 LAPS RACED **16,863 KM RACED** 4 SEASONS (2018-2021) (1 NON-COMPETING) **4 TEAMMATES (FERNANDO ALONSO, STOFFEL VANDOORNE, CARLOS SAINZ, DANIEL RICCIARDO.)**

McLaren were convinced that they had a driver who, though young, was mature enough to take the wheel of their F1 car, and in 2019 he was chosen to partner Carlos Sainz Jr.

It turned out not to be the most auspicious start to his F1 career, although 11th place was not to be sneezed at; Sainz had placed 15th on his maiden drive. A frustrating number of technical problems thwarted his efforts; engine troubles in Belgium, retirement in Mexico, power loss in Germany, suspension problems in Canada and a collision in Spain. 6th was the best finish he could manage that year.

McLaren kept the faith, nonetheless, and gave Lando a contract until 2022, so he was back in 2020, when, apart from engine trouble at the Nürburgring in Germany, he finished every race, unable, however, to improve on his podium 3rd place in Austria but claiming two 4th and two 5th places. He even out-qualified his teammate in eleven of the twenty-one races.

DRIVING STYLE

Lando's style is a work in progress and therefore still tricky to pinpoint. He can be extremely fast over one lap and controls his front and rear well.

He was pleased to have Daniel Ricciardo as his new teammate feeling that the Australian's presence helped him to improve his driving skills, providing him with someone against whom he could measure his progress.

There have been changes in the McLaren car, which for 2021 was the MCL35M, and Norris acknowledged that he needed to adopt a rather different driving style, try not to overdrive, commenting that Daniel Ricciardo's driving style might be more suitable to the new version of the car than his own in certain respects. As the season progressed, however, it turned out that Lando had a better grip on the car's requirements than Daniel. Not keen on understeer, preferring his car to be less stable at the rear, Lando had been described as a somewhat aggressive driver, whose degrees of confidence in qualifying or in a race, he says, change every year. In 2021, he thought, he was more confident in the races, a statement borne out by his 6th place in the World Championship results.

With Daniel Ricciardo as his partner for 2021, Lando claimed his second F1 podium at Imola, Emila Romagna, two more coming in the Monaco GP as he claimed 3rd place despite a penalty for having been judged to have forced Sergio Pérez off the track, and then Austria. He completed a McLaren one two in Italy after coming in second behind teammate Ricciardo after Verstappen and Hamilton crashed, with Hamilton lucky to emerge alive from his car wreck.

Although pushing hard for the points, Lando was still far from catching Verstappen and Hamilton, although at his young age, it will not be long before he becomes one of the drivers to beat.

PIE

GASLY

Pierre Jean-Jacques Gasly was born on the 7th of February 1996 in Rouen, France. His father is Jean-Jacques Gasly and his mother Pascale.

Pierre comes from a family of racing competitors. His father has competed in karting, rallying and endurance racing and his grandfather was also involved in karting.

Pierre's first experience of racing was at the age of six, and he came to befriend several other drivers who have since become famous in Formula One, such as Charles Leclerc and Esteban Ocon. Pierre's initiation into competitive karting came at the age of 10 in 2006 in the French Minime Championship. He came fourth in the competition the following year moving onto the French Cadet Championship in 2008 and then into the KF3 category where he was runner-up in the CIK-FIA European Championship.

Pierre progressed to the French F4 Championship 1.6-litre category in 2011 winning three races and gaining seven podiums.

In the Formula Renault Eurocup in 2012, he joined R-Ace GP, taking two podiums and finishing in 10th place. With the same team, he also entered the Formula Renault 2.0 Northern European Cup.

Title success finally came his way in 2013 when he joined Tech 1 Racing with three wins under his belt and five podiums.

Arden then hired him for the Red Bull Junior Team Development Program in 2014, where he drove in the Formula Renault 3.5 Series, when, claiming eight podiums, he was runner-up to Carlos Sainz Jr.

Pierre gained GP2 series experience at Monza when he replaced Tom Dillmann. It was not a smooth run with the DAMS team either, despite four podiums and three pole positions; he caused three collisions and finished in 8th place.

In May 2015, Pierre tested the Toro Rosso STR10 in Barcelona, switching to the Red Bull RG11 on day two, driving 203 laps. He was considered good enough by September to be officially named reserve driver for Red Bull Racing.

His competition luck changed with the Prema Powerteam in 2016, when he became champion for the GP2 Series, whilst he continued testing for Red Bull Racing and Scuderia Toro Rosso into 2017. And it was in 2017 that he got his first taste of the real thing, racing in F1 for the Scuderia Toro Rosso team, completing five of the races outside of the points, ending the season in 21st place.

PIERRE GASLY RACE STATS

86 GRAND PRIX 1 WIN (1.16%) **309 POINTS** 26 LAPS LED **3 FASTEST LAPS** 3 PODIUMS **15 RETIREMENTS** 5,383 LAPS RACED **22,829 KM RACED** 5 SEASONS (2017-2021) **7 TEAMMATES (CARLOS SAINZ, SEAN GELAEL, BRENDON HARTLEY, MAX VERSTAPPEN, DANIIL KVYAT, NAOKI YAMAMOTO, YUKI TSUNODA.)**

Driving for Red Bull Toro Rosso Honda in 2018, he now had a permanent seat, earning his first points in Bahrain, where he finished in a season-best 4th place. Pierre and teammate Hartley crashed in China after a misunderstanding, and Pierre concluded his full first season in 15th position.

Pierre was behind the wheel of the Aston Martin Red Bull Racing in the Red Bull RB15 for 2019, a year that brought him his first runner-up position in Brazil. Benefitting from a collision between Lewis Hamilton and Alex Albon, he managed to keep Hamilton at bay in a straight race for the finish line. He also claimed one 4th position, was 5th once and 6th twice that year, whilst suffering another collision, in Germany this time, and trouble with his suspension and driveshaft in Brazil and Azerbaijan.

Nonetheless, despite being demoted to Toro Rosso, the junior team, replaced by Alex Albon whilst Red Bull assessed Pierre's performance, the Frenchman was beginning to make his presence felt on the Grand Prix circuit and had worked his way up to 7th in the table by the end of the season and gained his highest tally of points, 95.

DRIVING STYLE

Pierre commented that he felt that his driving was "a bit too aggressive" earlier in the 2019 season, which adversely affected his ability to to adapt to the RB15, Red Bull's Formula 1 car. He cited tyre traction as one of the areas needing attention, which he needed to "get clean". There was also the problem of pushing the car hard, which, although this made the car whip around the course and paid dividends on occasions, often overheated the engine and tyres; "We know what happens with these tyres", he added. He has also worked on achieving more predictability and consistency in his drives. Pierre has shown that he possesses the essential competitive streak, showing fierce motivation and great race craft, pushing his cars to their limit at every race and offering feedback to his engineers that proves invaluable.

Unfortunately, Pierre's bad luck continued into 2020 when he was driving for the Scuderia AlphaTauri Honda team. A water leak, a collision, and gearbox trouble saw him forfeit three of the races. Nonetheless, his big moment arrived in Italy when he drove home ahead of the pack, resisting the late challenge by Carlos Sainz Jr,. to claim the winner's podium. There was still only a 10th place finish to his season however.

Another collision awaited him in 2021 in Styria, and he struggled to get into the top five with just one 3rd, 4th and 5th finishes and two 6th position finishes.

But Gasly has been commended for weathering the setbacks on the track and in his personal life, proving that he has the strength of character to fight back and possibly to surprise everyone and achieve his dream of competing amongst the top three drivers more often. Pierre ended the 2021 season in 9th place in the World Championship results.

Besides his native French, Gasly also speaks Italian and English.

CAR

SAINZ JR

C arlos Sainz Vázquez de Castro, known simply as Carlos Sainz or Carlos Sainz Junior, was born on the 1st of September 1994 in Madrid, Spain. He is the nephew of a rally driver, and his father, Carlos, has been World Rally Champion twice.

Carlos' karting career took off in 2008 when he won the KF3 Asia-Pacific title, also taking the runner-up position in the Spanish Championship. The following year he was again runner-up, this time in the European KF3 Championship, whilst emerging victorious in the Junior Monaco Kart Cup.

Racing in Formula BMW with the EuroInternational team in 2010, his talent became obvious when he was a guest driver at Sepang, coming in 2nd, 4th and 1st in his three races, results that brought him to the attention of the Red Bull Junior Team, where he joined their junior team programme. In 9 races, he secured 3 poles, 2 fastest laps and 2 wins.

He was also impressive in Formula BMW Europe, finishing the season on 4th place with 277 points.

Carlos moved up to Formula 3 in 2012 and signed with Arden the following year, which produced a season of mixed results.

For 2013, Sainz was announced as a test driver for Toro Rosso and Red Bull at Silverstone, whilst still racing in GP3, which again produced an unsatisfactory season. He also started driving in Formula Renault 3.5. His experience in that category was peppered with wins, retirements and races missed through other commitments.

With DAMS in 2014 he achieved greater success bringing in several victories, and then, in 2015, he finally made it to the F1 circuit driving for Scuderia Toro Rosso alongside Max Verstappen.

CARLOS SAINZ JR RACE STATS

141 GRAND PRIX 536.50 POINTS **17 LAPS LED** 1 FASTEST LAPS **6 PODIUMS** 27 RETIREMENTS **8,339 LAPS RACED** 37,369 KM RACED **8 TEAMMATES (MAX VERSTAPPEN, DANIIL KVYAT, SEAN GELAEL, PIERRE GASLY, NICO HÜLKENBERG, ARTEM MARKELOV, LANDO NORRIS, CHARLES LECLERC.)**

It was not the most auspicious start to a career, and he was plagued with car troubles, losing power on three occasions and experiencing problems with the brakes, wheels and electrics. He also withdrew from one race and received a 5 second penalty in another. Carlos didn't finish the Russian GP having crashed into the Tecpro barriers during the third free practice session. Going into the 13th turn he lost control of his car at the Sochi Autodrom and ended up in hospital for the night. That all left him in 15th position at the end of the season.

However, he started for Toro Rosso again in 2016 – only to experience more car problems; steering, a puncture, the suspension and a collision didn't help his chance to shine, though he managed three 6th place finishes. After the collision at the final race in Abu Dhabi, he had clawed his way to 12th position.

Hopes were dashed again in 2017 when the car gave him electrical and engine problems, but he was involved in three collisions and retired in Japan after a crash. Despite all of this, his was able to improve his standings and take 9th place after the final race.

By then, however, he was no longer with Scuderia Toro Rosso, having moved to Renault Sport Formula One Team in a Renault R.S.17 for the final four races after that crash in Japan. Carlos was now partnered with the experienced Nico Hülkenberg. Spinning the car in Mexico was not exactly an impressive exhibition of driving skill for his new team to watch, unfortunately.

Nico Hülkenberg also beat him in the table the following year when Carlos was 10th and Nico 7th, but at least he was managing the majority of his finishes between 5th and 10th position.

DRIVING STYLE

Carlos is less aggressive than other young drivers, and commented: "My driving style and the way I turn in, brake, carry speed through the corners in different places and different corner types is very different to last year" (with McLaren). Carlos is open to adapting his style to suit his new car and enjoying every minute of it.

Carlos Sainz is an intelligent and instinctive driver, one who possesses an extraordinarily sensitive feeling for his tyres and who demands more grip from them because he can keep them useful for longer than other drivers. He is continually thinking about how to thread through a race and gain points and this trait is now paying dividends. A calm temperament allows him to make considered decisions and to remain relatively unscathed by the pressures of bearing a famous name.

Ever eager to improve, Carlos Sainz has a combative spirit, a driver who will give his all to speed towards the checkered flag, and he does so with what has been described as a "finesse" that puts him on a par with Damon Hill and Jenson Button.

But for the new season came a new change as Carlos took the wheel of a McLaren, to replace Fernando Alonso, who had retired. Lando Norris was his new partner. Finally, Carlos was able to make a significant challenge to his competitors and came home on 6th place, well ahead of Lando, who was in 11th place at the end of the year. There was a large gap, however, between his 96 points and those of 5th placed Vettel with 240.

Carlos placed ahead of Lando again in 2020, retaining his 6th place but this time with an improved points tally of 105. His season had started well with a 5th place and then a 9th at the Austrian and Styrian Grands Prix; he achieved a career-best qualifying result of 3rd at the Styrian GP. He also set a new Red Bull Ring track record by achieving his fastest Formula One lap to date.

Carlos entered the team revolving door again in 2021 to take a seat with Scuderia Ferrari; at least the car troubles ceased. With the season more than half over, Carlos was driving well, even though he was having difficulty pulling in the points. But he had managed two podiums in his new steed having finished 2nd in Monaco and 3rd in Hungary and only placed outside of the number 10 spot twice. It may be that Carlos is finding his rhythm in a reliable car at last and that bodes well for his future. His 5th position at the end of the 2021 season bodes well for his future and makes him another young driver ready to endanger the big boys' domination.

KI
RÄIKKÖN

Kimi-Matias Räikkönen was born on the 17th of October 1979 in Espoo, Finland. Karting success started to come his way from the age of 10, although his first love was ice hockey, as it is for many people born in Scandinavia. He later explained his choice of racing as a career: "Because I didn't have to get up early in the morning."

By 1997, his climb towards F1 had begun, and he proved his ability by winning the Finnish Championship ICA for two consecutive years. The second year, 1998, he won two more championships beside the Finnish Championship ICA; the Finnish Championship Formula A and the Nordic Championship ICA.

Moving into the Formula Renault 2.0 UK Winter Series in 1999, he took 1st place in that championship also, in parallel with driving his kart in the Finnish Championship Formula A in which he came 2nd.

In the UK one year later, the year 2000, he was again in 1st place in the Formula Renault 2.0 at the age of 20. With a 57% win rate in the Formula Renault UK Championship and the British Formula Renault Winter series (i.e., 13 in 23 outings), it was inevitable that a Formula One team would show interest in the young driver.

The first team to bite was the Sauber Formula One Team in September 2000, when Räikkönen was given a test. To keep his name secret from potential rivals, Peter Sauber gave the young man the nickname of Eskimo, and once Eskimo had proven his worth after further tests, Sauber signed up the young man for the 2001 season.

KIMI RÄIKKÖNEN RACE STATS

F1 WORLD CHAMPIONSHIP 2007 **353 GRAND PRIX (4 NO STARTS)** 21 WINS (5.95%) **18 POLES** 1,873 POINTS **1,305 LAPS LED** 46 FASTEST LAPS **103 PODIUMS** 2 HAT-TRICKS **72 RETIREMENTS** 19,421 LAPS RACED **92,636 KM RACED** 16 TEAMMATES (NICK HEIDFELD, DAVID COULTHARD, PEDRO DE LA ROSA, JUAN-PABLO MONTOYA, ALEXANDER WURZ, FELIPE MASSA, LUCA BADOER, GIANCARLO FISICHELLA, ROMAIN GROSJEAN, JÉRÔME D'AMBROSIO, FERNANDO ALONSO, SEBASTIAN VETTEL, ANTONIA GIOVINAZZI, ROBERT KUBICA, MICK SCHUMACHER, CALLUM ILOTT)

Although doubts were expressed about the young Finn's lack of experience, he soon put paid to those by scoring a championship point in the Australian Grand Prix in 2001, his debut race. By the end of the season, Räikkönen and his teammate Nick Heidfeld had given Sauber a 4th place in the Constructors' Championship, its best ever position. Räikkönen placed 10th in the championship at the end of the season with nine points, just behind Heidfeld with 12.

The Nordic driver did even better the following year, when Kimi had been seduced to join McLaren for the 2002 season, his teammate now David Coulthard. Kimi finished in 6th place with 24 points and McLaren gained 3rd place in the Constructors' Championship.

In 2003, the Finn gave Michael Schumacher the fright of his life by finishing the season just two points behind the German. Along the way, Kimi won his first race in Malaysia, and clocked up several 2nd-place finishes.

In 2005, he again showed that he was a dangerous man to underestimate. With seven victories boosting his points tally, the season became an exciting tussle between himself and Fernando Alonso, who also claimed seven victories.

At the final chequered flag, however, after a season in which Kimi's engine had failed and a mistake had given Alonso an advantage, it was Alonso who took the championship, beating the Finn into 2nd place; 133 points to 112. Schumacher had been left far behind in 3rd with just 62 points.

Kimi stayed with McLaren for the 2006 season, despite his unease at its performance, but it wasn't an easy season with mistakes and retirements taking their toll, the result being that he could only take 6th place that year.

DRIVING STYLE

It goes without saying that all world champions are fast, and Kimi Räikkönen, of course, was no exception, and even spoken of as perhaps the fastest man of the early 2000s.

Although often considered to have a similar driving style to Michael Schumacher, Kimi was different to other champions in that he never adapted his driving style to the car, the car had to be adapted to his driving style and preferably with oversteer, having the back end slide out thus momentarily 'steering' the car.

Often let down by the cars he guided so smoothly around the circuit with a loose grip on the wheel, it's thought that he preferred those cars to be high revving. These characteristics also needed to be paired with a positive front end, the nose of the car solid in the apex of a curve enabling him to hit the floor with the throttle as fast as possible out of the curve. He was another master of the mid-curve direction change, eager to spend as little time going around it as possible, but also known for his ability to minimise tyre degradation.

Kimi decided that it was time for a change, and in 2007 he was seated behind the wheel of a Ferrari at the start of the season in Australia, gained pole position and went on to win the race.

What a year 2007 proved to be for Räikkönen. He added another five victories whilst being chased by both Lewis Hamilton and Fernando Alonso.

Following that first victory, however, it seemed as though he was going to lose out again that year thanks to a retirement and an accident in qualifying. Thus he missed out on points in two races. Together with 3rd and 4th place finishes, that left him 26 points behind Lewis Hamilton.

Everything changed at the French Grand Prix, which Räikkönen won, as he did the next race in Britain. Forced to retire in the European Grand Prix with car problems, he then came second in Hungary and Turkey and finally took another victory in Belgium. He was fortunate that Hamilton was out of the points after retiring in the penultimate race in China, which Räikkönen won.

The deciding race took place in Brazil; Kimi was lagging behind Lewis Hamilton by 7 points and Alonso by three. But he triumphed by overtaking Hamilton and race leader Felipe Massa and fetching another victory to beat Lewis to the title by one point.

Disappointed by the results of 2008 when he came 3rd, 23 points behind Hamilton, and 2009 when he came 6th, and unable to secure a seat with a team he felt had a chance of challenging for the championship, Kimi decided not to drive in the 2010 season. Instead he joined the World Rally Championship ending the season in 10th place. He stayed in the championship for the 2011 season as well.

After trying his hand at various US race meets, Räikkönen decided to return to F1, and on the 29th of November 2011, his return to Formula 1 was announced for 2012. He had signed a two-year contract with Lotus. By finishing the season in 3rd place, he showed that he had lost none of his skills in the intervening years.

However, after just one more season at Lotus and a 5th position, he was in the Ferrari seat for 2014, where he would stay until 2018. He came no closer than 4th until that final year when he again took 3rd place at the season's end.

From 2019, he joined Sauber, which then promptly changed its name to Alfa Romeo Racing, but after a good start, it became obvious that the Alfa Romeo Racing C38 was not going to bring in the awards, as the results deteriorated each year; 12th, 16th and 16th again for 2021, the year he caught the Covid-19 virus.

For Kimi, "The Iceman", as he is affectionately known, a man who belies his nickname by being known as "one of the warmest and friendliest people in the F1 paddock", his career was at an end, and he announced that he would leave F1 at the end of the 2021 season. At the age of 42, he was the oldest driver during the 2021 season (Yuki Tsunoda at 21 years of age was the youngest).

The man renowned for his laconic replies – who, when asked what he did the night before a race, replied: "I sleep" – is one of only five drivers to have taken over 100 podiums. Kimi's tally is 103.

Kimi Räikkönen is married to Minna-Mari "Minttu" Virtanen and the couple have a son and a daughter. True to his character, Kimi is involved in charity work but does so quietly and without media fuss.

Kimi Raikkonen of Finland driving the Alfa Romeo Racing C38 Ferrari, leaves the pitlane during final practice for the F1 Grand Prix of Abu Dhabi at Yas Marina Circuit on November 30, 2019

KIMI RÄIKKÖNEN HONOURS INCLUDE

DHL FASTEST LAP AWARD, 2007, 2008 AUTOSPORT RACING DRIVER AWARD, 2005 **FIA ACTION OF THE YEAR AWARD (FOR OVERTAKING 10 CARS ON HIS OPENING LAP AT THE PORTUGUESE GRAND PRIX), 2020** MOST WINS IN A DEBUT YEAR, 6, WITH FERRARI, 1990 **MOST PODIUMS, 9, AT THE SAME GRAND PRIX, HUNGARIAN, 2003, 2005, 2007, 2008, 2009, 2012, 2013, 2017, 2018**

Kimi Raikkonen of Finland driving the Alfa Romeo Racing C39 Ferrari during final practice for the F1 70th Anniversary Grand Prix at Silverstone on August 08, 2020

Kimi Raikkonen of Finland driving the Alfa Romeo Racing C41 Ferrari during the F1 Grand Prix of Azerbaijan at Baku City Circuit on June 06, 2021

Kimi Raikkonen of Finland and Ferrari drives during practice ahead of the Singapore Formula One Grand Prix at Marina Bay Street Circuit on September 19, 2014

DRIVERS IN 2021

Driver:	Country:	Start year:	Race Wins:	World Champion
Alonso, Fernando	Spain	2001	Yes	No
Bottas, Valtteri	Finland	2012	Yes	No
Gasly, Pierre	France	2017	Yes	No
Giovinazzi, Antonio	Italy	2017	No	No
Hamilton, Lewis	UK	2007	Yes	Yes
Kubica, Robert	Poland	2006	Yes	No
Latifi, Nicholas	Canada	2018	No	No
Leclerc, Charles	Monaco	2016	Yes	No
Mazepin, Nikita	Russia	2021	No	No
Norris, Lando	UK	2018	No	No
Ocon, Esteban	France	2014	Yes	No
Pérez, Sergio	Mexico	2011	Yes	No
Räikkönen, Kimi	Finland	2011	Yes	Yes
Ricciardo, Daniel	Australia	2011	Yes	No
Russell, George	UK	2017	No	No
Sainz, Carlos	Spain	2015	No	No
Schumacher, Mick	Germany	2020	No	No
Stroll, Lance	Canada	2017	No	No
Tsunoda, Yuki	Japan	2021	No	No
Verstappen, Max	Netherlands	2014	Yes	Yes
Vettel, Sebastian	Germany	2006	Yes	Yes

THE WORLD OF FORMULA ONE

> Lewis Hamilton after the Portuguese Grand Prix, 2020

It was 1950, it was England, it was Silverstone, it was the first Grand Prix World Championship. Since then, circuits have bloomed all across the globe, and since that first GP there have been 75 twisting and turning circuits on which the drivers could test their skills, from venerable Silverstone, still going strong today, to young upstart Portimão in the Algarve in Portugal that saw its first race in 2020.

Let's take a look at some of the tracks that have produced extraordinary world champions of the calibre of a Lewis Hamilton, Sebastian Vettel, Fernando Alonso or Michael Schumacher. Never to be forgotten, of course, Ayrton Senna and Juan Manuel Fangio, illustrious names from the mists of yesteryear. And the young drivers that may well take over from them at the top of the podium, Lance Stroll, Lando Norris, George Russell, Carlos Sainz or Charles Leclerc.

SILVERSTONE

Silverstone has changed since that first race, of course, won by Giuseppe Farina for Alfa Romeo, by the way. Now 5.891 km long (3.660 miles) and home to the British GP, it was once an RAF airfield and is subjected to powerful cross winds that make life tricky on the track and require drastic adjustments to braking distances. Silverstone is a fast circuit that includes the long Brooklands Straight and the Hanger Straight, which can see cars get up to speeds of 320 km/h (198.83 mph). It also boasts the tricky left-hand corner known as The Loop that makes drivers slow down to 95-85 km/h (59.03-52.81 mph). And it features the iconic Maggots and tight Becketts sections plus the dangerous Luffield, a right-hand hairpin and a third-gear curve. And then there's the exciting full throttle right-hander for

the Copse curve, allowing a minimum speed of 310 km/h (190 mph) on a dry surface. Not forgetting the 16th turn, Vale, where anyone mistiming their braking will be kicking up gravel.

The fastest lap ever recorded here was driven by Max Verstappen in a Red Bull RB16 on the 2nd of August 2020 in a time of 1:27.097 min. The outright lap record however goes to Lewis Hamilton for his 1:24.303 when he secured pole for the same race on the layout used since 2011. Hamilton also broke a 52-year-old record for most wins in the British Grand Prix by a Formula One driver when claiming his sixth win at Silverstone in 2019. The pit straight has now been named after him.

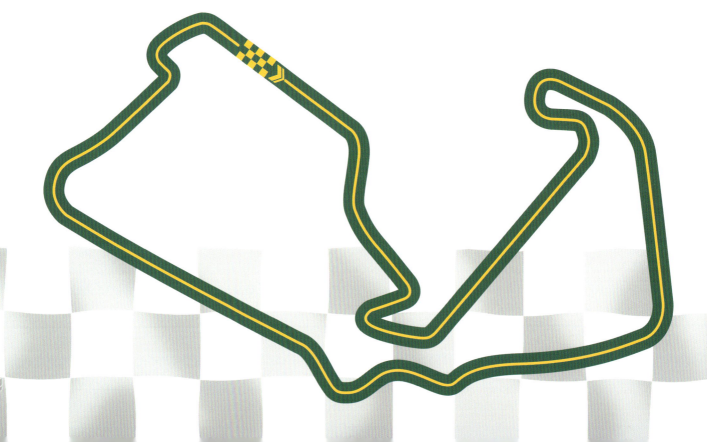

AUSTIN

A relative newcomer to receiving the F1 entourage can also be found in Austin, Texas, USA, one of the few tracks to run counter-clockwise; the Circuit of Americas.

Its 5.514 km (3.426 miles) track was first used in 2012, and it was Lewis Hamilton who took the honours that year around the 56 laps.

Fans recognise that some of the curves remind them of various other tracks such as the stadium corners at Hockenheim, the Silverstone Maggots-Becketts-Chapel sequence or Istanbul's four-left. As German architect and circuit designer Hermann Tilke helped in construction, a man who has designed many other tracks, Hockenheimring and Istanbul included, this is hardly surprising.

The circuit has an intense mix of slow corners and fast straights, perfect for an attempt at passing, followed by slow hairpin bends – one

of the most sinister of those arrives just after the start, presenting a considerable drop in elevation, to try and catch out any momentary lapse of concentration.

The Austin GP starts with a long uphill pull, an 11% gradient, and demands cool-headed reactions from the drivers and a lot of tyre grip, so plenty of excitement guaranteed. Never more so than on that long sprint between turns 11 and 12, where the cars can open up the throttle for just over 13 seconds and reach speeds of 315 km/h (195.73 mph) over 1.016 km (0.63 mile). Drivers have to be careful with gear selection, which will be affected by the prevailing winds, and a false decision could jeopardise an optimum exit from the straight.

Fastest lap recorded here was by Charles Leclerc on the 3rd of November 2019. He clocked up 1:36.169 min. Lewis Hamilton has won five of his eight races here, a record to date.

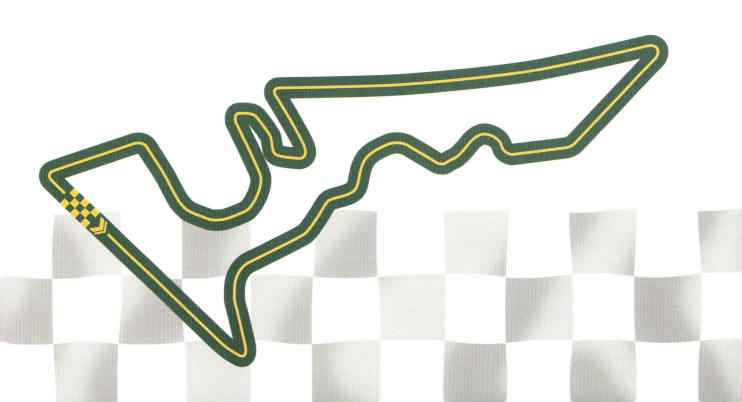

HUNGARORING

The circuit with just one true long straight, the pit lane, has been hosting F1 since 1986, when it became the first F1 GP behind the Iron Curtain.

It's located in Mogyoród, 20 km to the north-east of Budapest. It is still only race on the calendar to take place in the Eastern European countries. It is also the scene where two drivers, Nigel Mansell in 1992 and Michael Schumacher in 2001, claimed their World Championship titles. But the first man to claim a victory was Nelson Piquet after a spectacular slide into the lead around Ayrton Senna.

The track has known controversy, too, as when Schumacher almost squeezed Barichello against the pit wall in 2010 (for which he, uncharacteristically for him, apologised later).

Lewis Hamilton set the fastest racing lap here, along the 4.381 km (2.722 miles) track, completing the circuit in 1:16.627 minutes in 2020 in his Mercedes-AMG F1 W11 EQ Performance. Max Verstappen drove the fastest lap in 1:17.103 min. in his Red Bull RB 15 on the 5th August 2019. Drivers can hit 315 km/h (195.73 mph) along that start/finish straight as opposed to 280 and 285 km/h (177.09 mph) maximum for the other two on opposite sides of the circuit.

The Hungaroring is a difficult track, peppered with twists and turns. There are a few series of corners looped together, so the cars are set up for a downforce normally reserved for Monaco's streets, for example. As the straights are so short, attention to the chassis is paramount over raw horsepower. It's not everyone's first choice but many of the drivers enjoy the challenge and find that setting a good rhythm early on pays dividends.

Then a driver will enter that final turn at somewhere between 130-150 km/h (93.20 mph) and has to be be careful to reign in his enthusiasm, as he cannot simply brake, turn in and then sprint away. He has to hold the pedal in the corner and master any understeer balance before exiting perfectly lined up, he hopes, to take the flag after 70 laps of the track known as known as "Monaco without the glamour".

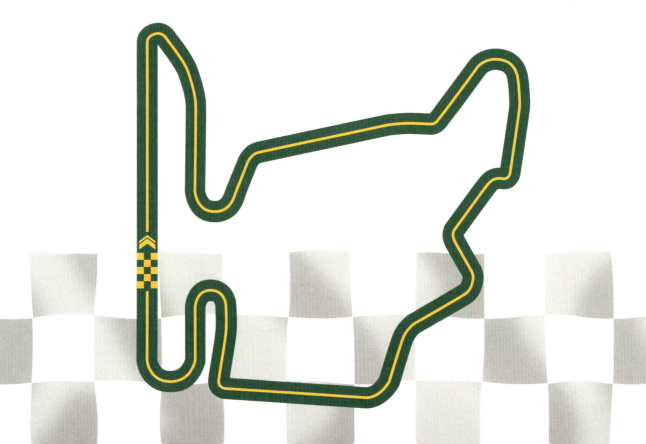

MONZA

The Italian circuit of Autodromo Nazionale Monza is now legendary, and the racing history that flows in its tailwind since its inception in 1922 is also legendary. Monza is a fast track, and speed carries danger alongside thrilling racing; the result has been the death of 52 drivers, three on one day in 1933, which is now known to historians as the "Black Day of Monza". Fortunately, no F1 driver has died there since Ronnie Peterson in 1978.

Hosting the Italian Grand Prix since the Formula 1 Championship first took place, (with the exception of Imola in 1980), it's length is now 5.793 km (3.600 miles).

The lap record is still held by Rubens Barichello, who clocked up a record speed of 1: 21.046 min. in his Ferrari F2004 on the 12th of September in 2004.

Monza, the shortest race of the season with its 53 laps, about 80 minutes, boasts four straights along which the drivers can really let rip with the throttle; on the pit straight, drivers can reach speeds of 350 km (217.47 mph) an hour, so the wing angles are amongst the smallest in Formula One and the downforce settings the lowest to ensure those fast straights can be taken at maximum speed. There are just 6 corner complexes.

The ability of the driver to judge the approach to the corner is paramount, as is clear from the pit lane straight; cars will be in eighth gear tearing towards the Variante del Rettifilo at well over 340 km/h (210 mph), drivers hoping to enter the chicane in first gear at 86 km/h (53 mph) to gain a clear exit in second gear at a mere 74 km/h (46 mph). They will then accelerate to 220 km/h (136.7 mph) into the long Curva Biassono leaving it behind themselves at over 325 km/h (201.9 mph). If they attempt to cut the chicane, they risk striking the kerbs, taking momentary flight and thus damaging the engine.

The Curva Parabolica corner, too, almost a U between two straights, demands smooth power delivery from the driver, as anything less can destabilise the car that will moving towards it at 335 or more km/h (208 mph).

It was Lewis Hamilton who recorded the fastest ever pole position lap in 2020 hitting 1:18.887 min.

MOST WINS. Michael Schumacher, 5
(1996, 1998, 2000, 2003, 2006)
Lewis Hamilton, 5
(2012, 2014, 2015, 2017, 2018)

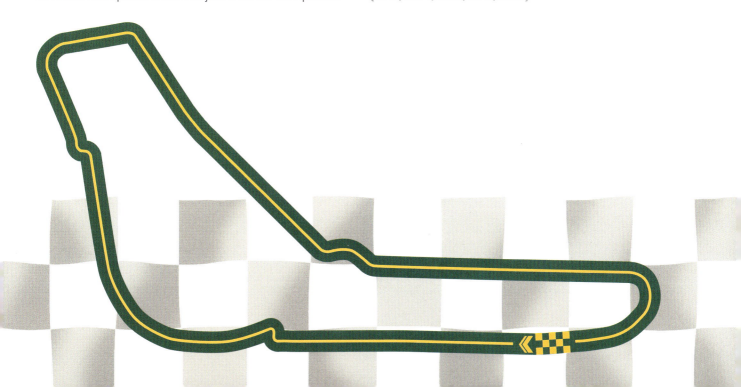

BARCELONA

Barcelona has witnessed F1 racing since being built in 1991, at what is now known as the Circuit de Barcelona-Catalunya, 20 km north-east of the city.

One of the more unpredictable tracks, the circuit is subjected to enormous variations in wind direction during the day making it impossible for the engineers to know exactly which circumstances the driver will be racing in later in the day; oversteer in the morning might become understeer in the afternoon. This lack of predictability can cause drivers to lose control, as happened in 2015 to Fernando Alonso.

Barcelona has been the scene of two Formula One debut wins; in 2012, Pastor Maldonado won the Grand Prix, and in 2016 Max Verstappen won his first Grand Prix at the track, setting a record for being the youngest driver to ever win a Formula One Grand Prix race – 18 years and 228 days.

The track has been through many layout variations in its history. It now has a length of 4.655 km, which were lapped in record time by Max Verstappen in 2021 in his Red Bull Racing RB 16 B when he covered the track in 1:18.149 min. (just besting Valtteri Bottas in his Mercedes W11 on the 17th of August 2020 at 1:18.183 min.). The Barcelona circuit is also a testing track for Formula One cars, and teams, and therefore drivers, can read it like an open book.

Throughout the 66 laps, the cars' tyres are put to severe tests by the very long corners. And, of course, there is that 1,047-metre-long pit straight (0.65 mile) to finish the lap around what is a bumpy track that makes it hard for tyres to grip firmly. In 2018 the track was a given new surface for the first time since 2004, thanks to MotoGP riders complaining about it and the difficulties in surface tyre grip.

The cars are taken around right-hand curves that almost take them back on themselves before having to reduce speed to 125 km/h (77.6 mph) for the sharp left at curve 5. Even more tricky is curve 10, which will force an even greater reduction of speed from 305 km/h (189.5 mph) to 95 km/h (59 mph), and the driver will be in first gear for the exit before accelerating up the hill putting huge stress on the tyres.

And if the slow chicane between corners 14 and 15 has been safely negotiated then the driver is just one 230-km/h-right-hand curve away (142.91 mph) from the pit lane straight and a chance of overtaking at over 300 km/h (186.4 mph).

MOST WINS: Michael Schumacher, 6 (1995, 1996, 2001, 2002, 2003, 2004)

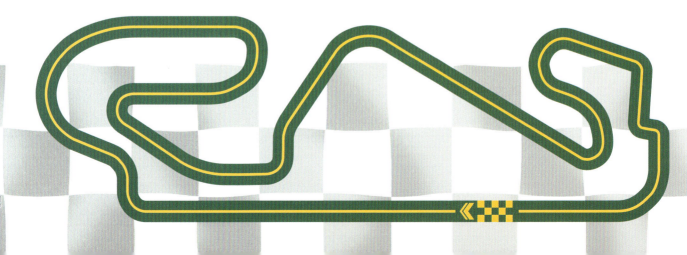

MONACO

The Grand Prix de Monaco, a unique occasion in the F1 year, one of the crown jewel races in what is known as the Triple Crown of Motorsport – the Monaco Grand Prix, the Indianapolis 500 and the 24 Hours of Le Mans.

Its uniqueness comes from the fact that the race takes place through the streets of Monaco, and its 3.337 km (2.074 miles) circuit includes tunnels, changes in elevation (over 30 metres) and tight corners, which, of course, means that the average speeds are far lower than those found on other tracks simply because the track itself is narrow and the closeness of the car to the walls presents an eternal danger for the drivers.

Monaco with its sun, sea and wealth has a glamour and abundance of beautiful people not to be found anywhere else on the Formula One circuits of the world. There have been many highlights at Monaco, some unfortunate, such as Paul Hawkins' Lotus car diving into the harbour in 1965, the year in which British driver Graham Hill set new lap records. In 1994, Sauber driver Karl Wendlinger from Austria crashed upon exiting the tunnel, hit the wall sideways and

his head struck a water-filled barrier leaving him in a coma for many weeks. In 2006, stewards accused Michael Schumacher of parking at the tight, 90-degree right turn La Rascasse so that his rivals could not attempt to take pole.

Despite minor alterations to the shape of the course and the additions of safety barriers so that trees and parked cars are no longer the only available means of coming to an abrupt standstill on the circuit, its 3.337 km (2.12 miles) track of 78 laps is so narrow that it's almost impossible to overtake, and the man who wins pole position in qualifying is usually the man who is first past the chequered flag in the race itself.

The feared corners – Sainte Devote, Mirabeau, The Grand Hotel Hairpin, the trademark tunnel and Anthony Noghés, are still there to send the imprudent driver to perdition. The Swimming Pool Complex is the one major alteration to the layout, thus allowing drivers to pass the Rainier III Nautical Stadium.

It's Brazilian driver Ayrton Senna who holds the record of six wins at the track, successfully negotiating that dreaded Grand Hotel hairpin, the

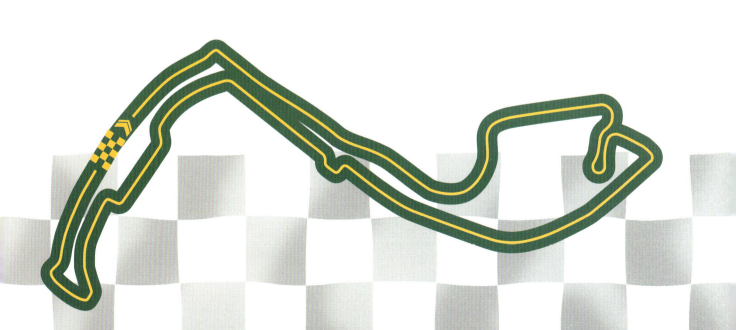

sharpest corner in the entire F1 network of tracks. The car reaches its lowest speed on any track, down to 44 km/h (27.3 mph). A slight miscalculation here, a locked brake, can be especially costly, for it can cause the car to strike the wall or the car in front.

The highest speed the cars can reach, twice, is some 295 km/h (183.3 mph); firstly, as they fire down the pit lane to the first turn, and then during the exit from the tunnel towards Nouvelle Chicane. Even there, the risk of overtaking is likely to involve the clashing of opposing car wheels.

Lewis Hamilton has completed this track in the fastest time achieving 1:12. 909 min. on the 23rd of May 2021

in his Mercedes W12. Monaco is, in fact, the shortest circuit of the year and is allowed to host the event despite not meeting current FIA requirements for a track to be a minimum of 3.5 km in length (perhaps it's not only history and pedigree that allow this unusual state of affairs to continue, but the arrival of some of the world's most glamorous stars and famous names, who lend the sport a few hours of fashionably dazzling glitz and glamour. That glamour, combined with the required driver bravery and razor-sharp driving skills, always makes this a race to remember.

**MOST WINS. Ayrton Senna, 6
(1987, 1989, 1990, 1991, 1992, 1993)**

Ayrton Senna of the McLaren-Honda racing team rounds a turn during the Monaco Grand Prix, 1988

SPA- FRANCORCHAMPS

The Circuit de Spa-Francorchamps in Belgium holds a special place in drivers' hearts. With its 20 turns and 7.004 km (4.352 miles), its vast elevation variations, gravel traps and unpredictable weather, this race is always a season highlight for fans. Once run along public roads – the first GP was held here in 1925 – safety concerns have seen its changing shape now ensconced in its own circuit area. Once feared by drivers thanks to the high speeds it could allow and corners taken at 180 km/h (111.84 mph), the track was changed in 1969 after drivers boycotted it. Deaths were not uncommon; two died in the 1960 race.

Following a death in an F2 race in 2019, gravel traps would be placed at La Source, Raidillon, Blanchimont, Les Combes and Stavelot, whereas some of the other corners would have their runoff areas expanded. Nonetheless, in 2021, during qualifying in heavy rain, Lando Norris oversteered his McLaren, slid into the Raidillon tyre barrier and spun five times as he twisted back across the track. He went to hospital for x-rays, but was able to race the following day.

One of the seven tracks in 1950 that constituted F1s first championship, there are three distinct areas to be coped with along this the longest of the circuits on the F1 calendar; the first sector involves the longest usage of full throttle in any F1 race, demanding low drag at a high top speed, and then there are corners to be taken at high speed in the middle section, and these need strong downforce with mechanical grip, which is essential in the third sector.

Spa tests the drivers to their limits thus producing some of the most exciting scenes in the F1 year. The tandem of the Eau Rouge and Raidillon corners in particular is thrilling when the cars hurtle through at full throttle. It's one of F1's "fabled corners"; in Jenson Button's words, "The feeling of the sweep uphill through the corners is just awesome, every time", whilst Lewis Hamilton thinks it to be the most exciting part of the track. "When you attack it flat out" he says, "when you get to the bottom of it, your insides

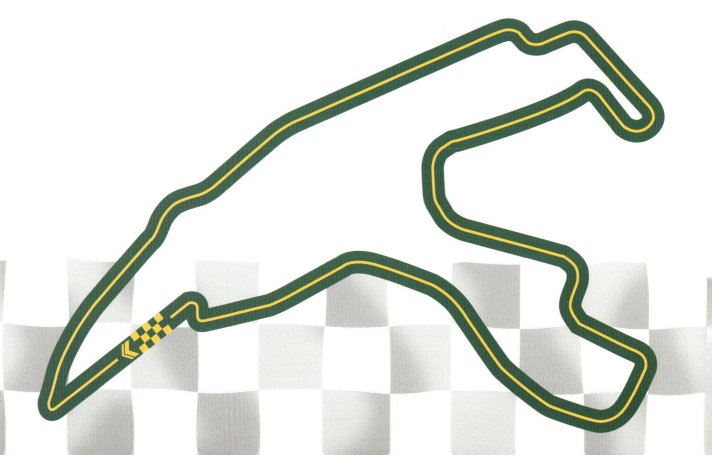

out of your mouth - which is quite exciting when you are going 200mph!" The corner has to be taken flat out and high downforce can increase the speeds. Losing control here is easy and that can lead to spectacular scenes, such as Jacques Villeneuve's crash in 1999. But the track will allow of speeds even faster, well over 330 km/h (205 mph) on the Kemmel Straight that follows the Eau Rouge and Raidillon sisters and almost those speeds between turn 15 and 17 (Blanchimont, which has also seen its share of accidents), and then 17 and the Bus-stop Chicane, which requires braking down to 110 km/h (68.3 mph).

So who has recorded the fastest lap on this trickiest of courses? The answer is Valtteri Bottas in 2018 in his Mercedes when he clocked up a time of 1:46.286 min.

Max Verstappen driving the Red Bull Racing RB16B Honda during qualifying ahead of the F1 Grand Prix of Belgium at Circuit de Spa-Francorchamps on August 28, 2021

NÜRBURGRING

Another of Formula One's legendary tracks, the Nürburgring in the Eifel area of Germany has had a chequered career of its own and used to include the infamous Nordschleife, a 20.8 km-long section of track (12.9 miles) that tormented drivers for 22 seasons. Jackie Stewart called it "The Green Hell" and it almost killed Niki Lauda in 1976, the year his Ferrari crashed following a rear suspension failure and he suffered horrific burns, his life saved by the swift actions of three other drivers – also the year the Nordschleife was abandoned. The tragic irony of the crash was that Lauda had tried to get the other drivers to boycott the race on the grounds that it was simply too dangerous but failed in the attempt to have the race abandoned.

Niki Lauda was the only driver ever to lap the Nordschleife in under seven minutes. A new circuit was constructed in 1985.

The race now covers 5.1 kilometres (3.1 miles), with the honour for the fastest lap time falling to Max Verstappen in 2020 in his Red Bull Racing RB16. Verstappen covered the circuit in 1:28.139 min. on the 11th of October 2020.

2020 saw the first F1 race at the track for seven years, (the first German GP took place in 1951) and the race was named the Eifel Grand Prix. The competition was notable for Lewis Hamilton's classic 91st F1 win – from second on the grid – with which he equalled Michael Schumacher's record number of victories. Schumacher has the section between Turn 7 and 10 named after him.

The track has three sections where the drivers can put the car through its paces; the first opportunity comes as they fire down the long pit straight before entering Castrol-S and the Mercedes Arena, where drivers need to get into second gear for the hairpin that follows at Turn 3, so they have to brake hard. The next chance for a brief period of top acceleration comes after the hairpin at Turn 7 into the Michael Schumacher-S, where the speed can hit the 300 km/h spot (186.4 mph) between Turn 9 and Turn 10.

Slowing sharply to enter the hard left RTL Curve and the Bit Curve almost immediately after, the cars have a final opportunity for a burst of throttle around the long sweeping curve between Turn 11 and the start of the NGK Chicane, swinging left at Turn 13. This chicane presents one of the trickiest situations on the track and momentary slow speed after almost constant acceleration; the cars must reduce velocity from around 300 km/h (186.4 mph) to just 90 km/h (55.9 mph) for the turn. A mistake here is costly, as coming out of this chicane into the Coca-Cola Curve for the last time presents the chequered flag just a few short metres away.

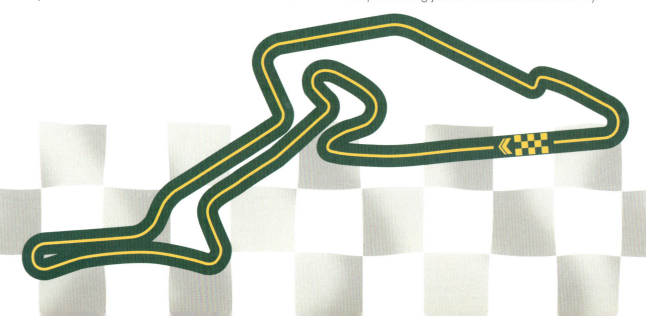

ABU DHABI

Some 30 minutes from Abu Dhabi, the capital of UAE, lies the F1 circuit of Yas Marina, a spectacular track purpose-built by German designer Hermann Tilke (who also designed the Sochi and Austin circuits) amongst others.

Opened in 2009, the year it hosted its first Formula One Grand Prix, the Yas Marina race has come to be Formula One's last event of the season.

With 21 turns, the fastest man over the 5.281 km (3.495 miles) circuit (changed from 5.554 km (3.451 miles) in 2021) is Lewis Hamilton, who covered the track's 55 laps in 1:39.283 min. in his Mercedes AMG F1 W10 EQ Power+ in 2019. Lewis Hamilton has also proven to be a master of the track's layout, recording victories on five occasions.

The 55 laps mean the drivers will cover 290.455 km (180.845 miles) in total. The circuit is notable not just for being one of the rare tracks that runs in an anti-clockwise direction, but also for the fact that it is a day-night race, starting at sunset, floodlights ensuring that the drivers can pass from light to darkness with relative ease. Also, the pit exit (the pit building has 40 air-conditioned garages to keep everyone cool from the roasting heat above) leads underground, and the drivers rejoin the circuit at Turn 3. Yas Marina contains long straights, a few tight turns to add to the tension, and sweeping corners.

Abu Dhabi has been the scene of dangerous incidents – Michael Schumacher only just avoided death in 2010 when a crash at the fifth corner caused Vitantonio Liuzzi's car to miss the German driver's head by a fraction.

The slowest moment arrives at the Turn 7 hairpin, where rear stability is paramount, so engine braking must be effective with drivers forced down to 70 km/h (43.5 mph). Reaction and re-acceleration must be spot on, as emerging from this turn, drivers are confronted with the longest of the straights, the 1.2 km run between turns 7 and 8. Drivers will approach Turn 8 at possible speeds of 330 km/h (205.05 mph), before heavy braking is required to take Turn 8 at 95 km/h (59 mph).

The straight is one of only two real opportunities to overtake, the second coming immediately after the tight left and right turns between turns 8 and 9.

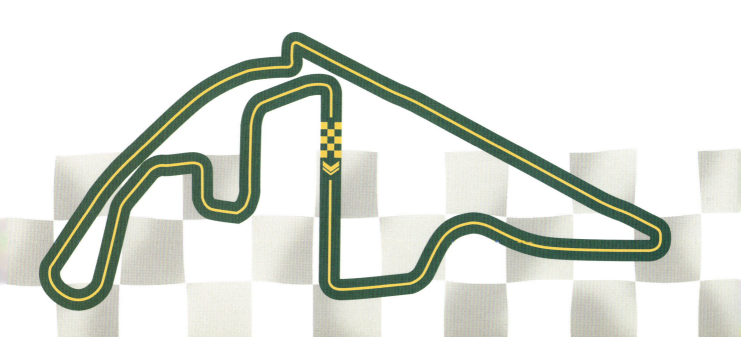

The sweeping left-hand curve between Turn 9 and Turn 11 can see speeds reach 325 km/h, (201 mph), which end abruptly when drivers are confronted with another sharp left and another sharp dip in speed to 105 km/h (65 mph).

From that point on, a series of left-hand turns taken in second or third gear mean that average speeds are fairly low and rear stability essential to keep the car 'glued' to the track. These turns lead to right-hand curves 15 and 16 taken flat out until Turn 21 and the main pit-lane straight.

A track that evokes a variety of responses from drivers – from tepid to ugly – Yas Marina's circuit is certainly a technical challenge.

MOST WINS: Lewis Hamilton, 5 (2011, 2014, 2016, 2018, 2019)

Lewis Hamilton of Great Britain driving the Mercedes AMG Petronas F1 Team Mercedes W11 on track during practice ahead of the F1 Grand Prix of Abu Dhabi at Yas Marina Circuit on December 11, 2020

PORTIMÃO

The newcomer to the calendar is the world-class Autodromo Internacional do Algarve, set in the hills in southern Portugal some 10 km north-west of the town of Portimão. Opened in 2008, it hosted the F1 event for the first time in 2020; the last time Portugal hosted an F1 race was in 1996 in Estoril.

Its 4.653 km (2.891 miles) track has drivers swooping up elevations and down again over its 66 laps – bringing comparisons to Spa or the old Nürburgring tracks – as drivers battle to conquer the race distance of 306.826 km (190.6 miles). Lewis Hamilton recorded the fastest lap time on the 25th of October 2020 at 1:18.750 and won the race both in 2020 and 2021. Hamilton, Bottas and Verstappen shared the podium after both races.

With excellent opportunities for overtaking along the wide track, the 15 terrific and flowing corners put the drivers' necks under considerable strain, and present some of the most testing and harsh breaking zones of all the F1 circuits, as it sends drivers swooping up and down the elevations. This track was of great significance for Hamilton, because it gave him his 92nd career victory, taking him past Michael Schumacher and giving him the

record of most Grand Prix wins ever.

There's a one-km sprint along the main straight, the Primeira, which dips downhill into the flat-out right-hand bend of Turn 2, and after the tight right-hand Turn 3 there's another chance of increasing speed as the drivers surge uphill to Turn 4 and give full throttle before slowing for Turn 5, the tight Torre Vip.

After leaving Turn 5, a series of left and right-hand curves will require good traction from the cars even as they then speed past Turn 9 – which has been named after Craig Jones, the World Supersport rider who was killed at Brands Hatch in the UK in a motorcycle crash in 2008 – again at full throttle.

And plunging down to the final right-turn Galp entry at full throttle into the main straight is a hard trick to master, keeping the car to right on entry without banking to maintain the best line for the hell-for-leather sprint to the chequered flag.

And with the track located in one of Europe's best tourist destinations on the sunny southern coast of Portugal, what more could an F1 fan ask for?

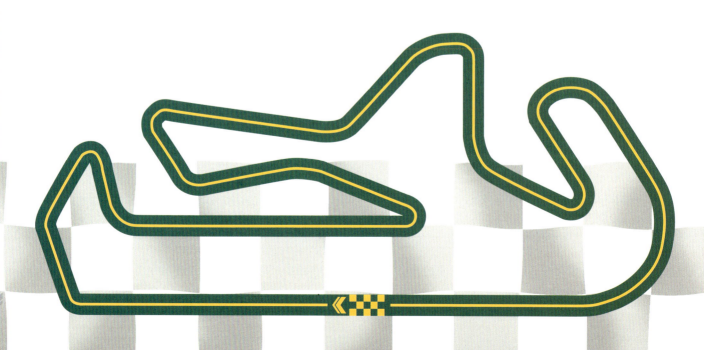

SUZUKA

Formula One's first Japanese Grand Prix took place in 1976, but subsequent races have been hosted at the Suzuka Circuit since 1987.

The track lies 150km east of Osaka, the only Formula One figure-of-eight circuit, and it also has a bridge spanning the track. Lewis Hamilton has claimed the fastest race lap around the around the 5.808 km (3.609 miles) in his Mercedes recording 1:30.983 min.

It has been the scene of many thrilling title-deciders, for Damon Hill, Mika Hakkinen and Sebastian Vettel, for example, and has also seen rivalries spill over into accidents; the clash between teammates Ayrton Senna and Alain Prost, who collided at the Casio Chicane in their McLarens in 1989, being just one such event.

The track is another that is unpredictable thanks to the, sometimes, extreme, weather conditions, but its high-speed straights, the series of turns, 3 to 7, known as The Esses, which the drivers enter at high speed and which demand switches of direction (Nigel Mansell crashed here in practice for the first 1987 race in his Williams-Honda), and the brake-juddering hairpin bend are sections of the track guaranteeing plenty of excitement that will quickly show who is master of his car.

The two-part right curve known as The Spoon Curve will catapult the drivers out to reach over 300 km/h (186.41 mph) towards the infamous turn 15, known as 130R, which puts the drivers under tremendous G-forces as they speed into the sweeping bend. It was here in 2005 that Fernando Alonso wrote history by overtaking Michael Schumacher at a moment when it seemed impossible to do so.

If the driver survives that high-velocity curve, he has to brake hard to bring the car back to 110 km/h (68.3 mph) for the Casio chicane, where high-profile incidents can always be expected, the tight right turn at 16 into the sharp left at 17 where it's tempting to overtake inside, and take advantage of Turn18 before opening the throttle for the race along the main straight.

An event that drivers look forward to, the fast and flowing nature of the Suzuka track – designed in 1962 by Dutchman John 'Hans' Hugenholtz – requires sharp driving thanks to its technical layout. This track rewards daring, strong, cool nerves, and it helps to have immense skill and talent.

All in all, 11 world champions have claimed their crowns here – and by the way, although Alain Prost took that 1989 title, Ayrton Senna got the upper hand in 1990.

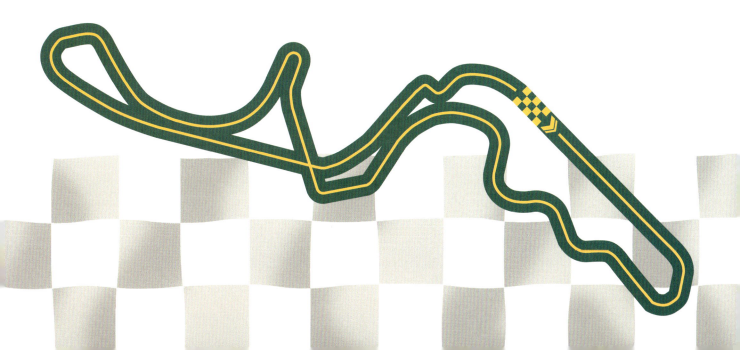

THE TEAMS

Some of the most prestigious and famous names in car and motor racing can be found amongst the teams in F1, all of them governed by the rules set by the Fédération Internationale de l'Automobile, the FIA. McLaren, Mercedes, Ferrari and Alfa Romeo are just a handful of world-renowned names.

And the team's constructors will compete to become the World Constructors' Champion, awarded to the constructor accumulating the most points based on the final position in which each of their two drivers passed the chequered flag at each Grand Prix.

Since 1950, 168 teams and 171 Formula One constructors have taken part in at least one of the World Championship Races. Many names have vanished into the mists of F1 history, those such as Bugatti, a legend in its own right, or Cooper-BRM, Hesketh and Jaguar.

Here are some of the lions of today's sport.

MCLAREN

Founded in 1966 by New Zealander Bruce McLaren – himself a Formula One driver, killed when his McLaren M8D crashed into an embankment at Goodwood on June 2nd 1970 – the team won its first Formula 1 victory at the 1968 Belgian Grand Prix and picked up its first world title in 1974 with Emerson Fittipaldi at the wheel. A second title came with British driver James Hunt in 1976. McLaren boasted four constructors world titles between 1984 and 1999 in the golden years when Alain Prost, Niki Lauda and Ayrton Senna took the wheel (in 1988, Prost and Senna won all but one race).

The low point in the company's history was undoubtedly the 2007 season when the team's chief designer, Mike Coughlan, was suspected of having stolen secret documents and McLaren were investigated by the FIA for possessing technical blueprints of Ferrari's car. McLaren was declared guilty and sanctioned by the FIA, which meant that the team, despite its lead in the constructors' standings, then lost all its points.

McLaren currently stand in third place in the all-time F1 team standings having 183 wins to their credit making them the second oldest active team and third most successful Formula One team behind Ferrari. In total, McLaren have won eight constructors' championships and twelve drivers' championships and have 6148.5 points in the all-time F1 team standings.

Now using Mercedes engines, having used Honda engines from 2015 to 2017, and after that changing to Renault engines, McLaren's two drivers for the 2021 season are Daniel Ricciardo and Lando Norris.

> Lando Norris of Great Britain driving the McLaren F1 Team MCL35M Mercedes stops in the Pitlane during final practice ahead of the F1 Grand Prix of Emilia Romagna at Autodromo Enzo e Dino Ferrari on April 17, 2021

MERCEDES

Competing for the first time in Formula One in 1954, Mercedes' first victory came at the French Grand Prix that year with Juan Manuel Fangio at the wheel. Fangio also took the Drivers' Championship in 1954 and 1955.

Mercedes–Benz decided to withdraw from motor racing following the Le Mans disaster in 1955. By then they had won two drivers' championships. (French driver Pierre Levegh was killed in the crash during the 1955 24-hour Le Mans motor race when he struck the car of Lance Macklin. Debris from the cars hurtle into the crowd killing 83 of the spectators and injuring another 180).

Mercedes did not compete in Formula One again until 1994, when the engines were used in partnership with McLaren with whom the company won one constructors' title and three drivers' titles. The partnership ended in 2009.

The Mercedes-Benz parent company then bought 45.1% of the Brawn GP team, and having rebranded the team as Mercedes GP Petronas Formula One team, were ready to complete in the Constructors' Championship. They hired two German drivers, Nico Rosberg and Michael Schumacher, who was returning to Formula One after a three-year break. Performances were way below expectations, however, and in 2012 the team officially designated itself the Mercedes AMG Petronas F1 team. For the first time in 57 years, Mercedes gained another win, in 2012 at the Chinese Grand Prix with Nico Rosberg at the wheel.

It was with the announcement that Lewis Hamilton would join Mercedes in the 2013 season that the new era of success opened up for the team, the year the V6 engine was used. The team's first Constructors' Championship win came at the Russian Grand Prix of 2013 as a works team, and with Hamilton taking the last race of the season, he secured the World Drivers' Championship, too, 67 points ahead of Rosberg.

The third Constructors' Championship arrived in 2016 when they won 19 of the 21 races.

But the year that will go down in the annals of Mercedes' F1 history as their most impressive to date is 2019, when the team took 15 of 21 Grands Prix, throwing in a record-breaking eight successive 1-2 results at the start of the campaign for good measure. They finished the season with the drivers and constructors titles in their hands for the sixth consecutive year.

The Mercedes W11 is considered to be perhaps the greatest F1 car ever produced and the team is as innovative as ever. The 'Dual Axis-Steering' system, although now banned, allowed for the front wheel toe to be altered when the driver pulled or pushed the steering wheel.

The latest version of the Mercedes is the Mercedes AMG F1 W12 E Performance, and the team sits at present in second place in the all-time teams standing table with 6347.64 points from 124 wins .

In total, Mercedes-Benz engines have garnered eight Constructors' Championship titles (2014, 2015, 2016, 2017, 2018, 2019, 2020, 2021) and thirteen Drivers' Championship titles.

» Lewis Hamilton of Great Britain driving the Mercedes AMG Petronas F1 Team Mercedes W11 stops in the Pitlane during the F1 Grand Prix of Italy at Autodromo di Monza on September 06, 2020

FERRARI

Ferrari was founded in 1929 by a former racing driver for Alfa Romeo, Enzo Ferrari. It has since become the most famous and the oldest Formula One team still participating in the event, although it withdrew from several races in the 1960s. Its prancing horse logo first appeared in 1932.

Scuderia Ferrari, the racing division of the company, achieved its first Formula One victory at the 1951 British Grand Prix in a car driven by Jose Froilán Gonzales. One year later, Ferrari claimed its 1st Drivers' Championship and from that point on it has continued to be the most successful F1 team and holds almost every Formula One record.

Having commenced racing 16 years before any other team still in competition with them, Ferrari has won more pole positions, more races, more fastest laps, achieved more 1-2 finishes, more podiums, and gained more points than any other team in the history of Formula 1.

Not overly concerned about winning the World Championship at the beginning of the 1970s, although they won races, once they hired Austrian driver Niki Lauda in 1974 that attitude changed, Ferrari became a name to reckon with. Lauda won the drivers' title in 1975 and Ferrari took the constructors' crown.

Despite winning the Constructors' Championship in 1982, it was a year to forget for Ferrari. The Canadian driver Jacques Villeneuve was killed during tests for the Belgian GP, and their other driver, Frenchman Didier Peroni, was involved in a terrible accident in practice in Germany ending his career.

Peroni died in a powerboat accident in 1987 at the age of 35. One of his sons, named Gilles in honour of his Canadian teammate, became an engineer with Mercedes.

Ferrari's drivers have been legends in their own right; Juan Manuel Fangio, John Surtees, Niki Lauda, Michael Schumacher and Kimi Räikkönen to name just a few. It has also supplied engines to other Formula One cars such as Sauber, Red Bull Racing, Scuderia Toro Rosso or Force India.

Without doubt, the most successful period for Ferrari was when Michael Schumacher was at the helm, although an accident at Silverstone in 1999 meant that he missed six races.

From then on however Ferrari became almost unstoppable. A third world title fell to Schumacher, who was the first Ferrari driver to win a title for 21 years. By 2004, Schumacher's five consecutive victories had given Ferrari its 14th drivers' title, five in a row, and its 14th constructors' title, the sixth in a row.

Ferrari's domination of the circuits, however, began to wane in 2005, and the last driver's champion was Kimi Räikkönen in 2007, and although the last Constructors' Championship was won in 2008, as of today, the team still holds the most the most, 16, and has produced the highest number of drivers' championship wins, 15, with the likes of Juan Fangio, John Surtees, Niki Lauda, Kimi Räikkönen and Michael Schumacher at the wheel.

Enzo Ferrari died in 1988 on the 14th of August at the age of 90, and between 2002 and 2004 Ferrari's latest and fastest model at the time was named after him.

The current drivers for the team are Carlos Sainz and Charles Leclerc.

Ferrari currently stands top of the all-time F1 team standings with 9304.79 points from 238 wins.

❯❯ Ferrari mechanics work on the car of Ferrari's Monegasque driver Charles Leclerc in the pit lane during a practice session at the Autodromo Internazionale Enzo e Dino Ferrari race track in Imola, Italy, on April 17, 2021

WILLIAMS

Williams, one of the 1990s most successful Formula One teams, was created when amateur driver and mechanic Frank Williams entered the racing car business, founding the "Frank Williams Racing Cars" team in 1966, racing his cars in the F2 Championship.

In 1969 he joined the F1 circuit with Piers Courage as his driver in a Brabham. Courage died during the Dutch Grand Prix in 1970, when Williams had switched to a De Tomaso chassis, which proved unreliable and too heavy. During the Dutch Grand Prix either the steering or the front suspension broke and Courage's car failed to take a high-speed bend. The driver was struck on the head by one of the car's front wheels and he died instantly.

Williams first championship double came in 1980, with the drivers' crown falling to them in 1981 and the constructors' title one year later. But further tragedy did not leave the team unscathed, either. Frank Williams was involved in a crash in 1986 when returning from an F1 test; he was left paralysed.

Another even greater tragedy awaited the Williams team in May 1994 when Ayrton Senna, three-times World Champion, was killed after his car crashed into a concrete barrier in the GP at San Marino.

But the roller-coaster fortunes of the team last saw success in 1996 and 1997 when, with mighty duo of Damon Hill and then Jacques Villeneuve, they claimed the world title and the constructors'

title making Williams one of the most successful F1 teams of the 90s. The roster of drivers has included such illustrious names as Britain's David Coulthard, Nigel Mansell, Jenson Button and, of course, Damon Hill, and the team has garnered seven Formula One drivers' championships; Alan Jones in 1980, Keke Rosberg in 1982, Nelson Piquet in 1987, Nigel Mansell in 1992, Alain Prost in 1993, Damon Hill in 1996, and Jacques Villeneuve in 1997.

At Monaco in 2021, Williams were on the grid for the 750th Grand Prix start, but when Claire Williams announced that she was leaving the team in 2020, the Williams team would be guided by the first team principal who was not a member of the Williams family, for the first time in 43 years since the company was founded. Following the Williams family's ending of their involvement in Grand Prix racing, the company was sold to Dorilton Capital to help bring in outside investment.

The team produced its worst results for two consecutive years gaining just one point in 2019. And in 2020 for the first time ever, Williams ended the season with no points at all.

However, since the arrival of managing director and team principal Jost Capito, William's fortunes have begun to turn around and they are now back earning points and even gaining the podium.

The Williams drivers for 2022 are Nicholas Latifi and Alex Albon

» Nico Rosberg of Germany and Williams waits in the pit during the F1 Grand Prix of Turkey at Istanbul Park on August 26, 2007

RED BULL

The Austrian Red Bull team has only been in the Formula One game since 2005 but in 16 years they have garnered four world titles, 75 Grand Prix wins to date and four constructors' titles. The team is now known as Red Bull Racing or Red Bull Racing Honda or even simply RBR.

The team rose from the ashes of driver Jackie Stewart's Stewart Grand Prix team, which was sold to the Ford Motor Company and later rebranded Jaguar Racing. The Jaguar team was taken over by Red Bull in 2004, not their first involvement in Formula One as they had been sponsors for Sauber between 1995 and 2004. David Coulthard was chosen as the main driver. The choice not only improved Coulthard's performance, but also brought in points and podiums for the team.

Swapping from Ferrari to Renault engines, which they then used between 2007 and 2015 but which were not powerful enough to combat the Mercedes engines, Red Bull now use Honda engines and have since become a force to be reckoned with in F1.

The first Formula One win came at the 2009 Chinese Grand Prix. At present they have won 75 races from the 326 Grand Prix starts and are on fourth place in the All Time F1 Team standings well above the Williams team, with 5,629 points to their credit.

Led by team principal Christian Horner, Red Bull has managed something other teams would dearly like to do, which is to become the most envied team on the grid, pushing the glamorous red Ferraris into the background. They are also fortunate with the presence of their talented driver Max Verstappen in the new RB16B, the last engine that Honda will produce. Red Bull will continue to maintain the engines until 2024. Red Bulls' boys in the pit can also be proud to claim the world's fastest pit stop, recording a time of 1.82 seconds at the Brazilian Grand Prix in 2019.

Impeded throughout 2019 and 2020 through lacking a reliable second driver, Sergio Pérez was brought in for 2021 to partner Max Verstappen and create a formidable team.

❯❯ Max Verstappen of the Netherlands driving the Aston Martin Red Bull Racing RB16 is helped into the garage by Red Bull Racing team members during qualifying ahead of the F1 Grand Prix of Abu Dhabi at Yas Marina Circuit on December 12, 2020

ASTON MARTIN

A name that has tradition and nostalgia behind it, though its track record in Formula One has not been particularly stellar. The team participated in Formula One racing in 1959, but following disappointing results they withdrew again the following year.

Despite speculation over several years that the team would return to F1, the consortium behind Aston Martin preferred to partner with an already existing team rather than start from scratch. Aston Martin, having sponsored Red Bull racing, has now entered the competition once more with the name being revived after the Racing Point F1 Team rebranded themselves as Aston Martin. This heralds a return to Formula One for Aston Martin as a constructor after a 60-year absence.

The team's main drivers for 2021 are Sebastian Vettel and Lance Stroll, and it was Vettel who gained the first podium for the team at the Azerbaijan Grand Prix. The two drivers are expected to be back behind the wheel for the 2022 season.

» Mechanics work on the car of Aston Martin's German driver Sebastian Vettel in the pit lane at the Autodromo Nazionale circuit in Monza on September 12, 2021

ALFA ROMEO

Another name that is rich with tradition and glamour, Alfa Romeo first entered the world of Formula One at the very first Grand Prix in Britain in 1950. They withdrew one year later, however, and did not return to the circuits until they began racing under the Sauber name. Sauber made its debut in 1993 taking its first points at the South African Grand Prix and a podium at the Italian Grand Prix one year later.

It wasn't until 2019 that Sauber announced that they would be known as Alfa Romeo Racing and the car would be the C38. Kimi Räikkönen, the 2007 World Champion, was brought in as the main driver alongside Antonio Giovinazzi.

The C38, however, proved to be extremely inconsistent, despite Kimi Räikkönen's efforts, and they gained 57 points at the end of the season for a P8 in the standings. Which was the position they ended the 2020 season with as well, whilst the two drivers managed just eight points between them. Both drivers gained points at Imola.

The rumour machine suggested that Alfa Romeo might be heading for a fast exit from F1 again, but for the moment that seems not to be the case because Valtteri Bottas is taking a seat with the team for 2022 replacing his countryman Kimi Räikkönen, who is retiring at the end of the 2021 season, to be teammate with Giovinazzi, who will be driving for the team for another season.

Alfa Romeo currently stand at 21st in the all-time F1 teams ranking table with 292 points from 172 Grands Prix.

≫ Marcus Ericsson of Sweden driving the Alfa Romeo Sauber F1 Team C37 Ferrari makes a pit stop for new tyres during the Formula One Grand Prix of France at Circuit Paul Ricard on June 24, 2018

HAAS

Haas is an American newcomer to the F1 circuits, having been founded by Gene Haas of NASCAR Cup Series fame in April 2014, and it's the first all-American-led F1 squad for three decades.

Their first race in F1 took place in 2016. The team's debut at the Australian Grand Prix, turned out to be quite a success with Romain Grosjean scoring eight points and a 6th finish. His partner in the team was Esteban Gutiérrez. At Bahrain, it was Grosjean who again put in an impressive performance to finish 5th. That was the last of the successful drives for that season and Grosjean's 29 points lead to an 8th place in the Constructors' Championship.

Kevin Magnusson coming in as second driver in the next season, 2017, led to the season being relatively successful with Grosjean finishing the season in 8th place and Magnuson on 10th and the team claiming 8th place in the constructors' title for the second year in a row.

With a new car, the VF−18 for the 2018 season, the team recorded the best season to date, the drivers coming in 4th and 5th in Austria and the team claiming 5th place in the Constructors' Championship.

With sponsorship problems plaguing them in 2019 there was little to celebrate that year with just 28 points; Haas finished with a ninth place in the Constructors' Championship.

Neither did 2020 prove to be any better; in fact Grosjean was fortunate to emerge from a collision in Bahrain that split his car into two before it burst into flames. Although the driver was hospitalised, for the burns on his hands, his life was probably saved by the halo head protection device.

Haas had two new drivers at the wheel for the 2021 season, Nikita Mazepin and the son of Formula One World Champion Michael Schumacher, Mick Schumacher. Beset once more by financial problems, the team decided to focus on the 2022 car, which has, unsurprisingly, meant that they have dropped down the all-time constructors' standings to 26th place with 200 points from 122 races.

Esteban Gutierrez of Mexico and Haas F1 in the Pitlane during practice for the European Formula One Grand Prix at Baku City Circuit on June 17, 2016

THE RACES

The driver rivalries add spice to the races making them unpredictable and exciting, adding to the intrinsically dangerous nature of the sport. Technology has changed the sport fundamentally since the early days of oil-stained garage floors. Every fan will have their favourite races, so it's impossible to do justice to them all in a single book. But to capture the flavour of some of those races that justify their places in the history of F1 as the most memorable, let's take a brief look at them, with a quick glance at some races that have receded into Formula One's thrilling and captivating past.

We can start with Brazil in 2003, a lunatic race that produced total chaos in a downpour that led to the race being started behind the safety car. In fact the safety car came out three times and the race was then restarted on lap 22, before reappearing for the fourth time when Jenson Button crashed badly at the Curva del sol. Yet Turn 3 caught out three drivers, Juan Pablo Montoya in his Williams-BMW, Antônio Pizzonia and then Michael Schumacher, who spun off on the wet surface.

David Coulthard in his McLaren-Mercedes was now in front being hunted down by Giancarlo Fisichella in his Jordan, Fernando Alonso and Coulthard's teammate Kimi Räikkönen. (Quote from the Scot: Kimi "...was either very fast or asleep").

But back in favour, it was the Ferrari of Rubens Barichello that took the lead from the Scot on lap 45, only for Räikkönen to take over at the front where it was then Barrichello's turn for Lady Luck to

kick him dramatically into the weeds when he ran out of fuel after a fuel sensor problem.

On Lap 54, Fisichella was next in line to grab the lead just before Webber's Jaguar-Ford Cosworth was involved in a mighty smash. Fisichella and Räikkönen immediately ran through the debris to help. Alonso caught one of the Jaguar's tyres causing him to crash as well. That was the end of the race, and Alonso was taken off to hospital. Following an official investigation, Fisichella was awarded the race, with Räikkönen and then

Alonso in his Renault taking 2nd and 3rd on the podium.

Brazil also hosted a spectacular GP in 2007, although that was a far more enjoyable event; this time Kimi Räikkönen was fighting rookie Lewis Hamilton for the championship. The British driver was thwarted by an engine problem that lost him ground, and even though he fought back brilliantly with grace and precision, the final 7th place left him just two points short, and the Finn took the top prize by just one point; Räikkönen 110, Hamilton 109.

Kimi Raikkonen of Finland and McLaren in action during practice for the Formula One Brazilian Grand Prix at Interlagos, Sao Paulo, Brazil on April 4, 2003

Jordan-Ford driver Giancarlo Fisichella of Italy in action during the Brazilian Formula One Grand Prix held on April 6, 2003 at Interlagos, in Sao Paulo, Brazil

Mark Webber crashed Jaguar during the Brazilian Formula One Grand Prix held on April 6, 2003 at Interlagos, in Sao Paulo, Brazil

Giancarlo Fisichella of Italy and Jordan makes his way through the crash debris during the Formula One Brazilian Grand Prix at Interlagos, Sao Paulo, Brazil on April 6, 2003

Leaping forward in time, there was the infamous but thrilling 2019 German Grand Prix held at Hockenheim in Germany, when the weather was so capricious that the drivers and teams were totally confused about tyres in the battle to keep their cars on the track. Just to emphasise the point, Lewis Hamilton visited the pits six times in his Mercedes!

For three laps, the safety car was in front, and from a standing start it was Hamilton and Bottas in the Mercedes-AMG Petronas cars who got away cleanly as the tyres filled the air with water spray. But Sergio Pérez's Racing Point 1 spun out of control on the second lap at turn 7 to bring the safety car out again. Then on lap 15, when Daniel Ricciardo's car experienced exhaust problems, there was a brief deployment of the virtual safety car, which enabled Nico Hülkenberg's Renault F1 Team car and Charles Leclerc's Scuderia Ferrari Mission Winnow pitstops for intermediates.

Verstappen in his Red Bull-Honda had another fright on lap 26 when he went into a spin on his slicks and only one lap later, the virtual safety car was again in use with Lando Norris's McLaren losing power forcing him to retire.

Fans were tense after yet another spin, from Lance Stroll's Racing Point 1 this time, which, fortunately, did not put him out of the race. But by the end of lap 28, it was Charles Leclerc's turn to push his luck too far and skid off and straight into the barrier bringing out the safety car one more time.

Hamilton was fortunate that he merely scraped the barrier after his skid, But most time was wasted in the pits because the crew were waiting for Bottas and not ready to fit a new tyre and front wing for Hamilton, which, in consequence, took 50 secs. To cap the bad news, Hamilton had entered the pits on the wrong side and was slammed with a 5-second penalty.

The skidding continued with the unlucky Nico Hülkenberg the victim at the end of lap 40 when he, too, skidded into the barrier. By the time most of the field had changed to slicks, Hamilton had dropped down to 12th place; but it got worse, because he did a complete pirouette on lap 53 when he hit a patch of water and the resultant pitstop put him right at the back of the field. Bottas would meet the same fate on lap 56 but was less lucky because he crashed into the barrier. It was Vettel who made the most progress working his way, finally, past Kvyat's Red Bull Toro Rosso Honda to take second place behind the cool head of Max Verstappen, who had seemed to be out of luck with that weak start and spent half his race unable to get out from behind the Alfa Romeo of Kimi Räikkönen.

But Verstappen pulled a rabbit out of the engine as the track slowly dried out, and he claimed his second win of the season. So the final results were: 1st, Max Verstappen, 2nd Sebastian Vettel, 3rd Daniil Kvyat, 4th Lance stroll and 5th Carlos Sainz Junior. Lewis Hamilton ended up in 9th place and Sergio Pérez took up the rear.

Max Verstappen of the Netherlands driving the Aston Martin Red Bull Racing RB15 on track during the F1 Grand Prix of Germany at Hockenheimring on July 28, 2019

There were two classic races in 2014 to delight the fans, one at the Hungarian Grand Prix and the other at the Bahrain Grand Prix, where Nico Rosberg and Lewis Hamilton were thrashing their cars around the circuit in a bitter "Duel in the Desert" to take the World Championship. Hamilton eventually emerged victorious even though Rosberg was using faster soft tyres, and a late safety car was brought on after a serious collision between Esteban Gutierrez and Pastor Maldonado that sent Gutierrez into a barrel roll, and caused Hamilton to lose his almost 10-second advantage.

Mercedes had decided not to give their drivers any team orders, and this led to a thrilling Grand Prix in which Rosberg and Hamilton swapped the lead and Hamilton's strategy of using soft tyres and keeping his mediums until the final lap meant that he was able to build a considerable lead. The Mercedes team became nervous at the increasing sharpness of the conflict between their two drivers and warned them to bring both cars home in one piece.

Despite Rosberg's attempts to overtake Hamilton, Hamilton's intelligent defence kept him in front all the way through to complete a Mercedes 1-2. The excitement was not only at the front, however, because Pérez beat Ricciardo by just 0.4 sec. and Nico Hülkenberg kept at bay a whole fleet of cars sweating behind him.

In Hungary another exciting race unfolded, but this time Lewis Hamilton managed just 3rd place behind Fernando Alonso and Daniel Ricciardo.

Thunderstorms and rain had made the track treacherous, and it was a hard decision for the teams between choosing intermediates or full rain tyres. More rain was forecast, erroneously, and made the teams even more nervous. As the spray made visibility tricky, Bottas managed to avoid it and stole the march on Vettel, whilst Hamilton's cold brakes caused him to spin on Turn 2. damaging his front wing. But he still sliced through field at one point to end up in front.

Grand Prix of Bahrain, Lewis Hamilton, Mercedes AMG Petronas F1 Team followed by Nico Rosberg, Mercedes AMG Petronas F1 Team, 06 April, 2014

A crash by Ericsson then brought out the safety car, which put an end to Rosberg's great start, and the unfortunate driver crashed again on lap 9.

Rosberg, gaining on Hamilton once more wanted to pass his teammate and the team asked him to do so. A shocked Hamilton refused and hung on for his 3rd-place podium.

In 2017 a nail-biting writing drama took place in Azerbaijan, which began with Sebastian Vettel in his Ferrari starting with a 12-point lead over Lewis Hamilton in the World Drivers' Championship. It was a race that took out Max Verstappen in his Red Bull Racing car when the engine failed on lap 12.

Valtteri Bottas and Kimi Raikkonen engaged in a merciless fight for supremacy before the safety car came out, at which point Vettel's Ferrari lost a section of its front wing when he drove into Hamilton's Mercedes. This led to Vettel blaming Hamilton for driving too slowly on purpose, pulling level with Hamilton, and deliberately smashing into the Mercedes – which, understandably, brought the German a time penalty.

Lap 20 then saw another collision between Sergio Pérez and Esteban Ocon in their Force Indias. The debris from the crash damaged Kimi Räikkönen's car and he was forced to retire, which meant that the safety car had to be deployed for a third time so that the track could be cleared.

The race seemed to be a four-car fight between Hamilton, Vettel, Ricciardo and Lance Stroll until on lap 29 Hamilton's headrest worked itself loose and he was forced into a pitstop on lap 31.

Eventually both Pérez and Räikkönen retired from the race and Bottas just managed to overtake Stroll on the final straight to sneak into 2nd position.

The outcome of all of this chaos was that Hamilton finished in 5th position, Vettel in 4th, but Daniel Ricciardo was able to claim his 6th Formula One win and Lance Stroll was proud to take his maiden F1 podium, the first Canadian to do so since 2001 and the era of Jacques Villeneuve. He was also the second youngest driver to gain the podium.

Red Bull Racing's Australian driver Daniel Ricciardo celebrates after the Hungarian Formula One Grand Prix at the Hungaroring circuit in Budapest on July 27, 2014

For 2018, opinion was fairly unanimous that the United States Grand Prix was the one to have seen that year.

After qualifying, it seemed that the Mercedes of Lewis Hamilton and Sebastian Vettel in his Ferrari were going to be competing for the honours. But Räikkönen kept Hamilton out at the start to roar into the lead, and Vettel found himself in a spin early on while duelling with Daniel Ricciardo, which condemned him to a final 4th at the finish. Lance Stroll then struck Fernando Alonso causing a dramatic crash during the first lap and Ricciardo flipped the bird at his Red Bull RB14 when it gave up the ghost on lap 9.

Räikkönen showed enormous cool-headed decision-making on lap 12 to hold off a determined Hamilton before putting in a fast pit stop of 2.3 seconds for soft compound tyres.

With Lewis Hamilton having difficulty keeping pace in the Mercedes and losing time when the team delayed his second pitstop, it was Kimi Räikkönen in his Ferrari who took advantage of his opponents' difficulties managing to keep ahead of Max Verstappen, who had threaded his way through to the 2nd place from 18th on the grid. He eventually finished 2nd as Räikkönen took the flag having had a nail-biting battle to keep Hamilton from claiming the second place.

Räikkönen's one-stop strategy had paid off, and he was rewarded with his first Grand Prix win since the Australian Grand Prix in 2013, and this was the first time that the Circuit of the Americas had seen a Ferrari victory. With no safety car and no bad weather, strategy and skill were on show here, allowing a thrilling battle between Hamilton, Verstappen and Räikkönen to unfold. This race is worth its reputation because Räikkönen drove superbly to fight off two mighty opponents, a terrific victory exactly 15 years and 212 days after his last win in the 2003 Malaysian GP. It also ended a record-breaking 113-race void without a win. A win that a great many would have wished for a driver who has gained an adoring, appreciative fanbase all around the world.

Mercedes AMG Petronas F1 German driver Nico Rosberg races on the wet track during the third practice session ahead of the US Formula One Grand Prix at the Circuit of The Americas in Austin, Texas, on October 24, 2015

⌃ Lewis Hamilton of Great Britain and Mercedes GP celebrates with the team in the pit lane after winning the United States Formula One Grand Prix and the championship at Circuit of The Americas on October 25, 2015

Of course, we can't leave this section without the two best races of the 2020 and 2021 seasons.

2020. Well, as usual the contenders crowd around, but I think we can't go far wrong by choosing the Grand Prix at Sakhir in Bahrain, the 1034th Grand Prix, which took place on the 6th of December 2020, a Sunday. Sakhir has 87 laps, each circuit being three 3.543 km in length. The result at the end of the race was surprising.

Lewis Hamilton had tested positive for Covid-19 and was devastated to have to miss the race. His seat in the Mercedes was taken by George Russell. And George wanted to make his mark, which he did by taking off from the front row like a bat out of hell to take the lead at Turn 1. Teammate Valtteri Bottas was forced into 2nd place, and the battle began between Russell and Bottas in their Mercedes, with Leclerc, Verstappen and Sergio Pérez behind them.

Verstappen lasted no longer than lap 4 thanks to Leclerc shoving into Pérez sending him into a spin, thus dispensing with Verstappen, who struck the barrier in his avoidance action and had to retire, as did Leclerc at the same time. Pérez fared little better either, having to go in for repairs, which dropped him down to 18th and last position in the field. Little did he know, but he was about to make one of the most remarkable comebacks in F1 history.

Russell began to increase his lead over his teammate, chased by Carlos Sainz Junior and Lance Stroll. Pérez, meanwhile, was biting his way back into the reckoning and by lap 20 had reached 10th position. The virtual safety car had to be brought out on lap 54, and both Sainz and Daniel Ricciardo were caught on the hop, because the virtual safety car period was shorter than they had anticipated. There was more confusion by lap 61 when the Williams car left its front wing at the final turn and the virtual safety had to be called once again.

And then, at lap 63, the two Mercedes were due

Sergio Perez of Mexico driving the Racing Point RP20 Mercedes on track during the F1 Grand Prix of Sakhir at Bahrain International Circuit on December 06, 2020

to go to the pit, but radio confusion led to Russell being sent out with front tyres intended for Bottas, which meant Russell was now guilty of an infringement. And Bottas was left sitting in the pit for almost 30 seconds, only to be sent back out without new tyres. So Russell had to come back into the pit again.

There was now a chance opening up for Pérez, Esteban Ocon and Lance Stroll, who took advantage of the Mercedes' error to leave Bottas in 4th position and Russell in 5th.

Russell, however, was not to be so easily beaten, and by lap 73, he had thrust himself back into 2nd position and was challenging Pérez for the leadership. Bottas was struggling with worn tyres and had soon fallen back to 9th, at which point Russell was in a strong position, challenging to take the race. Lap 78, however, and a puncture in his rear left tyre forced him back into the pit yet again. Undaunted, he showed his metal by firing himself

from the 14th to 9th position gaining points for the fastest lap of the race, 55.404 seconds, a world record F1 time, because it was the first occasion that a fastest race lap had been completed in under 60 seconds throughout the 70 years of Formula One racing history.

With just six laps to go, Pérez was ahead of Ocon by 8.6 sec., Stroll by 9.8 sec., Sainz by 11 sec., and Ricciardo by 11.8 sec. Only a direct lightning strike was going to stop him. It didn't.

So even with his record speed lap, Russell still couldn't prevent Sergio Pérez from taking his first Grand Prix victory after 190 Grands Prix, followed onto the podium by Esteban Ocon for Renault and then Lance Stroll, who had taken third place in his Racing Point BWT Mercedes. It was also Ocon's first F1 podium. A heartwarming sight.

2021 turned out to be a season to remember as well. George Russell became one of the season's

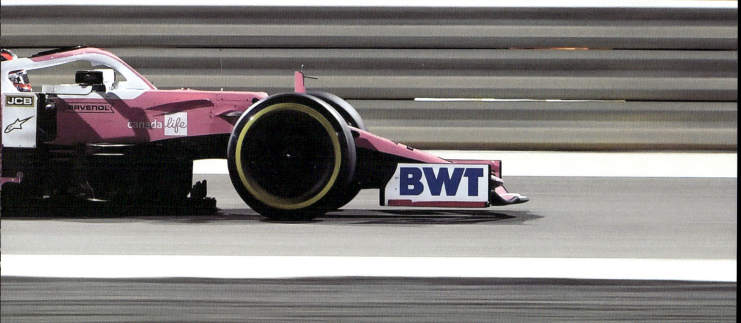

shooting stars, and his crash with Valtteri Bottas at Emilia Romagna was perhaps just a very bright if odd, symbolic signal that he was about to take over as Lewis Hamilton's teammate.

Mr. Sebastian Vettel, having changed to Aston Martin, gained his first podium for the new team, whilst at the Hungarian Grand Prix. Fernando Alonso put in a storming performance to hold off Lewis Hamilton. And, of course, we can't forget Lando Norris, the speedy new star in the F1 firmament, who pulled in three podiums and pressurised the big boys, Hamilton and Verstappen.

Impossible to choose in a season of thrills and spills, but we've picked out the Russian Grand Prix at the Sochi Autodrom on the 26th of September 2021 for one reason; that being, of course, that Britain's Lewis Hamilton became the first man to achieve 100 Grands Prix wins, whilst at the same time retaking the championship lead. And also because a sterling performance by another British driver, Lando Norris, almost caused a sensation.

Hamilton had a fight on his hands to get that record, with young Lando Norris taking his first Formula One pole position and George Russell achieving a faster qualifying time than Lewis, meaning the two were sandwiched in between the McLaren-Mercedes of Lando Norris and the McLaren-Mercedes of Daniel Ricciardo, 5th on the grid.

Norris was unable to hold his advantage for long, because Carlos Sainz Jr was in the lead from Turn 2. Hamilton found himself in trouble when Fernando Alonso overtook him at the start. Norris fought back to retake the lead on lap 13, and there he stayed for most of the race until the rain set in.

Hamilton decided to get into the pit for intermediate tyres, a decision that paid off on lap 51 when Norris started to aquaplane and Hamilton took advantage to snatch the lead, leaving Norris to finally end the race in seventh position. The race, however, proved that Norris was going to be a man to watch in the future.

But mention does have to be made of the 2021 British Grand Prix held on the 18th of July 2021 at the famous and venerable Silverstone circuit. This race will forever be remembered for the incident that involved the two top contenders for the championship title, Lewis Hamilton and a revitalised Max Verstappen.

For a while, it seemed as though Verstappen was going to run away with the title and Mercedes'

 Fernando Alonso of Spain driving the Alpine A521 Renault leads Max Verstappen of the Netherlands driving the Red Bull Racing RB16B Honda during the F1 Grand Prix of Russia at Sochi Autodrom on September 26, 2021

domination of the previous seasons had waned. Lewis Hamilton, however, had other ideas.

In qualifying at Silverstone, Lewis was ahead of Verstappen in his Red Bull Racing-Honda, who was squeezed between Hamilton and his Mercedes teammate Valtteri Bottas. The situation was reversed in the sprint qualifying classification when Max Verstappen came in ahead of Lewis Hamilton.

When the lights went out on the day, Hamilton was faster and had drawn up level with Verstappen, and the two men were competing fiercely with each other on every single term, one besting the other as they approached the seventh turn.

It was then that Hamilton accelerated his Mercedes faster than Verstappen's Red Bull as they left the turn, but as they approached the ninth corner Hamilton was determined to take the advantage. The two cars collided and Verstappen slipped sideways into the gravel trap outside the track, hitting the tyre wall and having the rubber stripped from his right wheel rim.

Even though at the time the stewards put the main blame on Hamilton, subsequent reviews have more than exonerated him from blame, and Verstappen was released from hospital later that night once it had been confirmed that his injuries were not serious. The collision meant that Hamilton had to pit and serve a 10-second time penalty, but he swiftly left the McLaren of Norris behind him and Bottas was told to let Hamilton past, which he did.

Despite needing repairs to his car, Hamilton fired around the track to chase Leclerc in the lead, who was, unfortunately suffering from momentary losses of power, which meant that the gap between him and Hamilton was a mere 1.5 seconds. But with Vettel having retired, Kimi Räikkönen suffering a spin in his Alfa Romeo on lap 49, Pérez' strategy of trying to beat Hamilton by putting on new soft tyres failing and Norris suffering from a right tyre issue that lost him time emerging from the pit lane, all attempts to halt the British driver were to no avail. Hamilton took Leclerc on lap 50 with 2 laps to go and the 1st place podium was his.

Norris was finally left to finish the race in 4th position, behind Bottas in 3rd and Charles Leclerc in 2nd place in his Ferrari. It was once again the extraordinary driving of Lewis Hamilton and his Mercedes that gave him another top of the podium.

Red Bull, were, naturally, out for a fight on their driver's behalf, but with the benefit of calmer reflection after the race, it was obvious to almost everyone that Red Bull had a very weak case to pursue, if, indeed, they had any case at all.

Finally, of course, the last race of the season that saw the championship decided between Lewis Hamilton and Max Verstappen.

With both drivers on 365.5 points at the start of the race, Lewis Hamilton was dominant throughout, leading the pack until the safety car was brought out following a crash by Nicholas Latifi. Confusion and frustration then befell many of the drivers at the decisions taken by the race director to restart the race, which, after the safety car had left the track, led to Verstappen taking the lead on the final lap having pitted for new tyres. It was a sorry way to end the season and left many people bewildered as to what had taken place, and not least engendered an uneasy sense that Hamilton had been robbed of victory by a technical error.

 Race winner Lewis Hamilton of Great Britain and Mercedes GP celebrates on the podium during the F1 Grand Prix of Russia at Sochi Autodrom on September 26, 2021

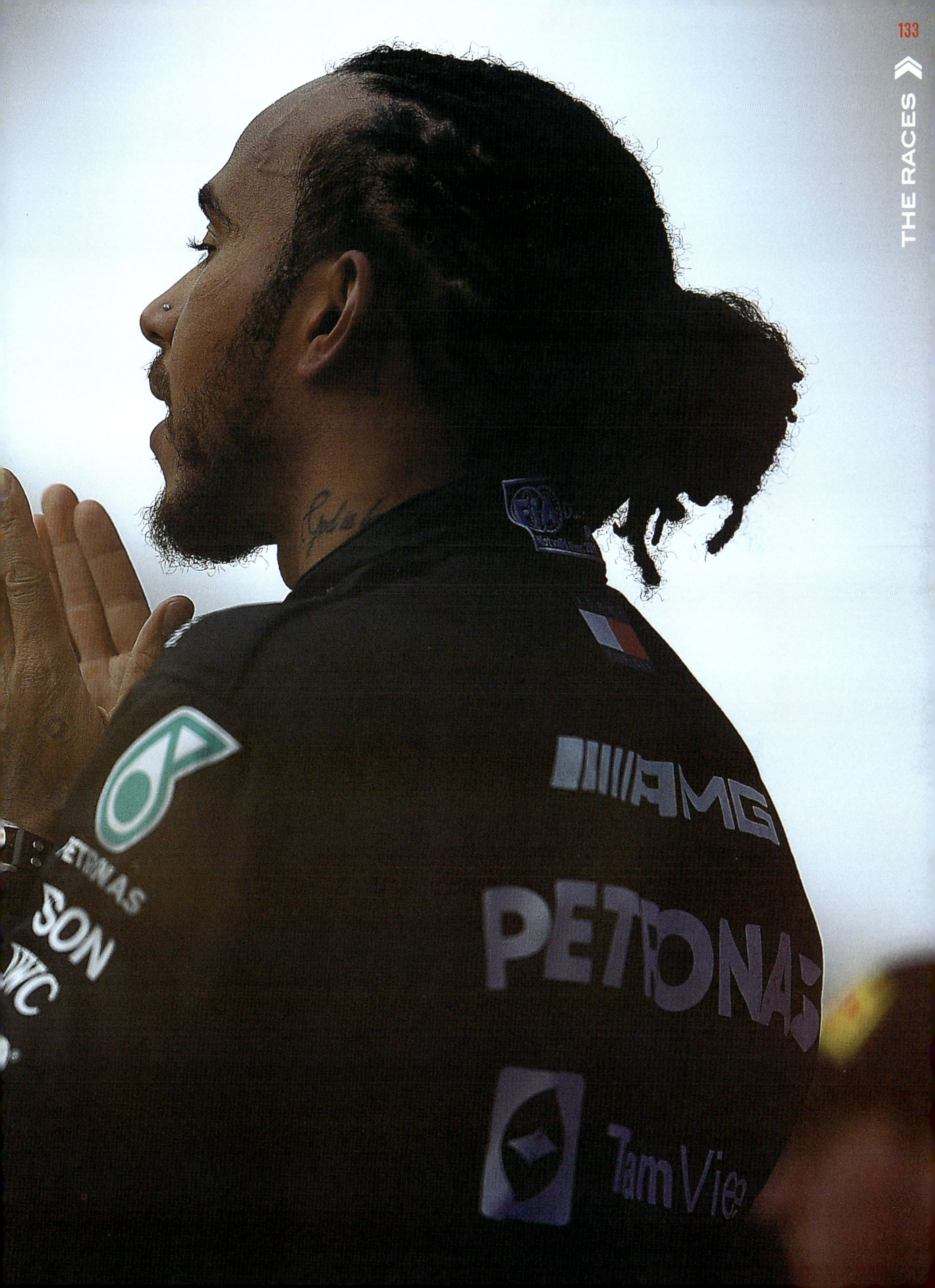
AMG

CONSTRUCTOR
STANDINGS

The FIA, the Fédération Internationale de l'Automobile, is responsible for awarding The World Constructors' Championship to the most successful constructor in the F1 competition during the season, the winner decided by using a points system calculated on individual Grand Prix results. Points scored by the driver are amassed for a particular constructor in each race.

The article governing the FIA Sporting Regulations state that the constructor designs certain parts of the car – survival cell, the front impact structure, the roll structures and bodywork – described in what is known as Appendix 6. The constructor will name the engine or the chassis.

Should two different companies make the chassis and the engine, then the constructor will be assumed to be both companies acting in unison, with the name of the chassis constructor written before that of the engine constructor; McLaren-Mercedes for example.

The F1 season concludes with the FIA Prize Giving Ceremony for the Constructors' Championship. Vanwall were the first winners of the F1 Constructors' Championship in 1958. Now in its 62nd season, only 15 chassis constructors – 170 chassis constructors have entered the F1 Grands Prix – have won the Championship. With 16 victories to celebrate, Ferrari has won the highest number of World Constructors' Championships. Quite a long way behind them in second position is Williams having won nine championships, and with eight titles McLaren takes third place.

Ferrari also heads the table as an engine manufacturer with 16 titles, although as Renault has 12, Ford has 10, Mercedes has nine with six for Honda, the competition is fierce.

Mercedes have dominated since 2014, with World Championship driver Lewis Hamilton partnered by Nico Rosberg, Valtteri Bottas or George Russell. And apart from one season, 2018, they secured the championship on each occasion with at least three races still left to run. 2021 proved no different with Mercedes securing another championship.

CHASSIS CONSTRUCTORS, WINNERS OF WORLD CONSTRUCTOR'S CHAMPIONSHIP:

NAME	TOTAL WINS	SEASONS
Ferrari	16	1961, 1964, 1975, 1976, 1977, 1979, 1982, 1983, 1999 2000, 2001 2002, 2003, 2004, 2007, 2008
Williams	09	1980, 1981, 1986, 1987, 1992, 1993, 1994, 1996, 1997
McLaren	08	1974, 1984, 1985, 1988, 1989, 1990, 1991, 1998
Mercedes	08	2014, 2015, 2016, 2017, 2018, 2019, 2020, 2021
Lotus	07	1963, 1965, 1968, 1970, 1972, 1973, 1978
Red Bull	04	2010, 2011, 2012, 2013
Renault	02	2005, 2006
Cooper	02	1959, 1960
Brabham	02	1966, 1967
Vanwall	01	1958
BRM	01	1962
Matra	01	1969
Tyrrell	01	1971
Benetton	01	1995
Brawn	01	2009

THE CONSTRUCTORS ACTIVE IN 2021 ARE AS FOLLOWS:

Swiss team Alfa Romeo	1950–1951, 1979–1985, 2019–2021
Italian team AlphaTauri	2020–2021
French team Alpine	2021
British team Aston Martin	1959–1960, 2021
Italian team Ferrari	1950– 2021
American team Haas	2016– 2021
British team McLaren	1996–2021
German team Mercedes	1954–1955, 2010–2021
Austrian team Red Bull	2005 -2021
British team Williams	1978 -2021

2021 DRIVER STANDINGS:

1.	Max Verstappen	Red Bull	395.5 points
2.	Lewis Hamilton	Mercedes	387.5 points
3.	Valtteri Bottas	Mercedes	226 points
4.	Sergio Pérez	Red Bull	190 points
5.	Carlos Sainz	Ferrari	164.5 points
6.	Lando Norris	McLaren	160 points
7.	Charles Leclerc	Ferrari	159 points
8.	Daniel Ricciardo	McLaren	115 points
9.	Pierre Gasly	AlphaTauri	110 points
10.	Fernando Alonso	Alpine	81 points
11.	Esteban Ocon	Alpine	74 points
12.	Sebastian Vettel	Aston Martin	43 points

13. **Lance Stroll** — Aston Martin — 34 points
14. **Yuki Tsunoda** — AlphaTauri — 32 points
15. **George Russell** — Williams — 16 points
16. **Kimi Räikkönen** — Alfa Romeo — 10 points
17. **Nicholas Latifi** — Williams — 7 points
18. **Antonio Giovinazzi** — Alfa Romeo — 3 point
19. **Mick Schumacher** — Haas — 0 points
20. **Robert Kubica** — Alfa Romeo — 0 points
21. **Nikita Mazepin** — Haas — 0 points.

2021 CONSTRUCTOR STANDINGS:

1. **Mercedes** — 613.5 points
2. **Red Bull** — 585.5 points
3. **Ferrari** — 323.5 points
4. **McLaren** — 275 points
5. **Alpine** — 155 points
6. **AlphaTauri** — 142 points
7. **Aston Martin** — 77 points
8. **Williams** — 23 points
9. **Alfa Romeo** — 13 points
10. **Haas** — 0 points

F1 CHAMPIONS LISTED BY YEAR:

YEAR	DRIVER	TEAM	WINS	POINTS
2021	Max Verstappen	Red Bull Honda	10	395.5
2020	Lewis Hamilton	Mercedes	11	347
2019	Lewis Hamilton	Mercedes	11	413
2018	Lewis Hamilton	Mercedes	11	408
2017	Lewis Hamilton	Mercedes	9	363
2016	Nico Rosberg	Mercedes	9	385
2015	Lewis Hamilton	Mercedes	10	381
2014	Lewis Hamilton	Mercedes	11	384
2013	Sebastian Vettel	Red Bull Renault	13	397
2012	Sebastian Vettel	Red Bull Renault	5	281
2011	Sebastian Vettel	Red Bull Renault	11	392
2010	Sebastian Vettel	Red Bull Renault	5	256
2009	Jenson Button	Brawn-Mercedes	6	95
2008	Lewis Hamilton	McLaren–Mercedes	5	98
2007	Kimi Räikkönen	Ferrari	6	110
2006	Fernando Alonso	Renault	7	134
2005	Fernando Alonso	Renault	7	133
2004	Michael Schumacher	Ferrari	13	148
2003	Michael Schumacher	Ferrari	6	93
2002	Michael Schumacher	Ferrari	11	144
2001	Michael Schumacher	Ferrari	9	123
2000	Michael Schumacher	Ferrari	9	108
1999	Mika Häkkinen	McLaren–Mercedes	5	76
1998	Mika Häkkinen	McLaren–Mercedes	8	100

1997	Jacques Villeneuve	Williams–Renault	7	81
1996	Damon Hill	Williams–Renault	8	97
1995	Michael Schumacher	Benetton–Renault	9	102
1994	Michael Schumacher	Benetton–Ford Cosworth	8	92
1993	Alain Prost	Williams–Renault	7	99
1992	Nigel Mansell	Williams–Renault	9	108
1991	Ayrton Senna	McLaren-Honda	7	96
1990	Ayrton Senna	McLaren-Honda	6	78
1989	Alain Prost	McLaren-Honda	4	76
1988	Ayrton Senna	McLaren-Honda	8	90
1987	Nelson Piquet	Williams-Honda	3	73
1986	Alain Prost	McLaren-Tag	4	72
1985	Alain Prost	McLaren-Tag	5	73
1984	Niki Lauda	McLaren-Tag	5	72
1983	Nelson Piquet	Brabham-BMW	3	59
1982	Keke Rosberg	Williams-Ford Cosworth	1	44
1981	Nelson Piquet	Brabham-Ford Cosworth	3	50
1980	Alan Jones	Williams-Ford Cosworth	5	67
1979	Jody Scheckter	Ferrari	3	51
1978	Mario Andretti	Lotus-Ford Cosworth	6	64
1977	Niki Lauda	Ferrari	3	72
1976	James Hunt	McLaren-Ford Cosworth	6	69
1975	Niki Lauda	Ferrari	5	64.5
1974	Emerson Fittipaldi	McLaren-Ford Cosworth	3	55
1973	Jackie Stewart	Tyrrell-Ford Cosworth	5	71
1972	Emerson Fittipaldi	Lotus-Ford Cosworth	5	61
1971	Jackie Stewart	Tyrrell-Ford Cosworth	6	62
1970	Jochen Rindt	Lotus-Ford Cosworth	5	45
1969	Jackie Stewart	Matra Ford Cosworth	6	63
1968	Graham Hill	Lotus-Ford Cosworth	3	48
1967	Denny Hulme	Brabham-Repco	2	51
1966	Jack Brabham	Brabham-Repco	4	42
1965	Jim Clark	Lotus-Climax	6	54
1964	John Surtees	Ferrari	2	40
1963	Jim Clark	Lotus-Climax	7	54
1962	Graham Hill	BRM	4	42
1961	Phil Hill	Ferrari	2	34
1960	Jack Brabham	Cooper-Climax	5	43
1959	Jack Brabham	Cooper-Climax	2	31
1958	Mike Hawthorn	Ferrari	1	42
1957	Juan Manuel Fangio	Maserati	4	40
1956	Juan Manuel Fangio	Ferrari	3	30
1955	Juan Manuel Fangio	Mercedes	4	40
1954	Juan Manuel Fangio	Maserati Mercedes	6	42
1953	Alberto Ascari	Ferrari	5	34.5
1952	Alberto Ascari	Ferrari	6	36
1951	Juan Manuel Fangio	Alfa Romeo	3	31
1950	Nino Farina	Alfa Romeo	3	30

CHAMPIONSHIP DRIVER STATISTICS:

DRIVER	WINS	TITLES	POINTS	SEASONS
1. Lewis Hamilton	103	7	4165.5	2008, 2014, 2015, 2017, 2018, 2019, 2020
2. Michael Schumacher	91	7	1566	1994, 1995, 2000, 2001, 2002, 2003 2004
3. Juan Manuel Fangio	24	5	277.64	1951, 1954, 1955, 1956, 1957
4. Alain Prost	51	4	798.5	1985, 1986, 1989, 1993
5. Sebastian Vettel	53	4	3053	2010, 2011, 2012, 2013
6. Jack Brabham	14	3	265	1959, 1960, 1966
7. Jackie Stewart	27	3	360	1969, 1971, 1973
8. Niki Lauda	25	3	420.5	1975, 1977, 1984
9. Nelson Piquet	23	3	485	1981, 1983, 1987
10. Ayrton Senna	41	3	614	1988, 1990, 1991
11. Alberto Ascari	13	2	140.14	1952, 1953
12. Jim Clark	25	2	274	1963, 1965
13. Graham Hill	14	2	289	1962, 1968
14. Emerson Fittipaldi	14	2	281	1972, 1974
15. Mika Häkkinen	20	2	420	1998, 1999
16. Fernando Alonso	32	2	1957	2005, 2006
17. Nino Farina	5	1	127.33	1950
18. Mike Hawthorn	3	1	127.64	1958
19. Phil Hill	3	1	98	1961
20. John Surtees	6	1	180	1964
21. Denny Hulme	8	1	248	1967
22. Jochen Rindt	6	1	109	1970
23. James Hunt	10	1	179	1976
24. Mario Andretti	12	1	180	1978
25. Jody Scheckter	10	1	255	1979
26. Alan Jones	12	1	206	1980
27. Keke Rosberg	5	1	159.5	1982
28. Nigel Mansell	31	1	482	1992
29. Damon Hill	22	1	360	1996
30. Jacques Villeneuve	11	1	235	1997
31. Kimi Räikkönen	21	1	1869	2007
32. Jenson Button	15	1	1235	2009
33. Nico Rosberg	23	1	1594.5	2016
34. Max Verstappen	20	1	1557.5	2021

DRIVERS WITH THE MOST POLE POSITIONS:

DRIVER	SEASONS	NUMBER OF POLES
1. Lewis Hamilton	2007-2021	103
2. Michael Schumacher	1991-2006, 2010-2012	68
3. Ayrton Senna	1984-1994	65
4. Sebastian Vettel	2007-20201	57
5. Jim Clark	1960-1968	33

6.	**Alain Prost**	1980-1991, 1993	33
7.	**Nigel Mansell**	1980-1992, 1994-1995	32
8.	**Nico Rosberg**	2006-2016	30
9.	**Juan Manuel Fangio**	1950-1951, 1953-1958	29
10.	**Mika Häkkinen**	1991 to 2001	26

DRIVERS LEADING THROUGHOUT EVERY RACE:

1. **Lewis Hamilton** — 23 races
2. **Ayrton Senna** — 19 races
3. **Sebastian Vettel** — 15 races
4. **Jim Clark** — 13 races
5. **Jackie Stewart/ Michael Schumacher** — 11 races
7. **Nigel Mansell** — 9 races
8 **Alberto Askari/ Alain Prost/ Nico Rosberg** — 7 races

LIST OF CIRCUITS SINCE 1950:

	Circuit	COUNTRY AND START YEAR.	NUMBER OF RACES HELD
1.	**Adelaide Street Circuit**	Australia 1985	11
2.	**Aïda**	Japan 1994	2
3.	**Ain-Diab Circuit Casablanca**	Morocco 1958	1
4.	**Aintree Motor Racing Circuit Aintree**	United Kingdom 1955	5
5.	**Anderstorp Scandinavian Raceway**	Sweden 1973	6
6.	**Austin Circuit of the Americas**	USA 2012	9
7.	**Avus Automobil-Verkehrs und Übungsstraße**	Germany 1959	1
8.	**Bakou Baku Street Circuit**	Azerbaijan 2016	5
9.	**Barcelona Circuit de Catalunya**	Spain 1991	31
10.	**Brands Hatch**	United Kingdom 1964	14
11.	**Bremgarten**	Switzerland 1950	5
12.	**Buenos Aires Autodromo Juan y Oscar Gálvez**	Argentina 1953	20
13.	**Caesars Palace**	USA 1981	2
14.	**Clermont-Ferrand Circuit de Charade**	France 1965	4
15.	**Dallas Dallas Fair Park**	USA 1984	1
16.	**Detroit**	USA 1982	7
17.	**Dijon-Prenois**	France 1974	6
18.	**Jeddah**	Saudi Arabia 2021	1
19.	**Donington Donington Park**	United Kingdom in 1993	1
20.	**East London Prince George Circuit**	South Africa 1962	3
21.	**Estoril Autódromo Fernanda Pires da Silva**	Portugal 1984	13
22.	**Fuji Fuji international Speedway**	Japan 1976	4
23.	**Hockenheim Hockenheimring**	Germany 1970	37
24.	**Hungaroring**	Hungary 1986	36
25.	**Imola Autodromo Internazionale Enzo e Dino Ferrari**	Italy 1980	29
26.	**Indianapolis Indianapolis Motor Speedway**	USA 1950	19
27.	**Interlagos Autodromo José Carlos Pace**	Brazil 1973	38
28.	**Istanbul Istanbul Park**	Turkey 2005	9

29. Jacarepagua Autódromo do Rio de Janeiro	Brazil 1978	10
30. Jarama	Spain 1968	9
31. Jerez de la Frontera	Spain 1986	7
32. Kuala Lumpur Sepang International Circuit	Malaysia 1999	19
33. Kyalami	South Africa 1967	20
34. Le Castellet Paul Ricard High Tech Test Track	France 1971	17
35. Le Mans Circuit Bugatti	France 1967	1
36. Long Beach	USA 1976	8
37. Losail Circuit International de Losail	Qatar 2021	1
38. Magny-Cours Circuit de Nevers Magny-Cours	France1991	18
39. Melbourne Albert Park	Australia 1996	24
40. Mexico City Autódromo Hermanos Rodríguez	Mexico 1963	20
41. Monaco	Monaco 1950	67
42. Monsanto	Portugal 1959	1
43. Mont-Tremblant	Canada 1968	2
44. Montjuïc Park	Spain 1969	4
45. Montréal Circuit Gilles Villeneuve	Canada 1978	40
46. Monza Autodromo Nazionale di Monza	Italy 1950	71
47. Mosport Park Mosport International Raceway	Canada 1967	8
48. Mugello Autodromo Internazionale del Mugello	Italy 2020	1
49. New Delhi Buddh International Circuit	India 2011	3
50. Nivelles Complexe Européen de Nivelles-Baulers	Belgium 1972	2
51. Nürburgring	Germany 1951	41
52. Österreichring	Austria 1970	18
53. Pedralbes	Spain 1951	2
54. Pescara	Italy 1957	1
55. Phoenix	USA 1989	3
56. Portimão Autódromo Internacional do Algarve	Portugal 2020	2
57. Porto Circuito da Boavista	Portugal 1958	2
58. Reims Circuit de Reims-Gueux	France 1950	11
59. Riverside Riverside International Raceway	USA 1960	1
60. Rouen-les-Essarts	France 1952	5
61. Sakhir Bahrain International Circuit	Bahrain 2004	18
62. Sebring Sebring International Raceway	USA 1959	1
63. Shanghai Shanghai International Circuit	China 2004	16
64. Silverstone	United Kingdom	56
65. Singapore Marina Bay Street Circuit	Singapore 2008	12
66. Sochi Sochi International Street Circuit	Russia 2014	8
67. Spa-Francorchamps	Belgium 1950	54
68. Spielberg Red Bull Ring	Austria 1997	17
69. Suka Suka international Racing Course	Japan 1987	31
70. Valencia Valencia Street Circuit	Spain 2008	5
71. Watkins Glen Watkins Glen International	USA 1961	20
72. Yas Marina	UAE 2009	13
73. Yeongam	South Korea 2010	4
74. Zandvoort Circuit Park Zandvoort	Netherlands 1952	31
75. Zeltweg Zeltweg Flugplatz	Austria 1964	1
76. Zolder Circuit Terlaemen	Belgium 1973	10